As long as there is
breath in your body,
THERE IS
STILL HOPE

As long as there is breath in your body, THERE IS STILL Hope

Releasing the Power of Hope

Rosalind Tompkins

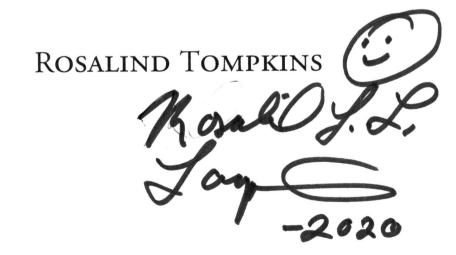

–2020

This is a work of creative nonfiction. The events herein are portrayed to the best of the author's memory. While all the stories in this book are true, some names and identifying details may have been changed to protect the privacy of the people involved.

This work is designed to provide accurate and authoritative information with regard to the subject matter covered. This information is given with the understanding that neither the author nor the publisher is engaged in rendering legal, professional advice. Since the details of your situation are fact dependent, you should additionally seek the services of a competent professional.

Biblical quotations are from the King James Version (KJV), the Berean Study Bible, the New Living Translation (NLT), or the New International Version (NIV).

Hebrew and Greek definitions are from *The New Strong's Exhaustive Concordance of the Bible*.

English definitions are taken from *Webster's Encyclopedic Unabridged Dictionary* Deluxe Edition and *Merriam-Webster's Collegiate Dictionary*, Tenth Edition.

Editorial work and production management by Eschler Editing
Cover design by Laks Mi, Gerard Hamdani, and Kenneth Ndung'u
Interior print design and layout by Kimberly Kay
eBook design and layout by Marny K. Parkin.

Published by Scrivener Books, and Think Hope Press

First Edition: March 2019

ISBN 978-1-7336519-8-1

Other Inspirational Books by Rosalind Tompkins:

As Long as There Is Breath in Your Body, There Is Hope
Rare Anointing
You Are Beautiful: Unlocking Beauty from Within
What Is It? Defining, Finding, and Obtaining Your It
Nimble Anointed Words Empower (N-AWE)

Original poetry included in the book is written by Rosalind Tompkins

CONTENTS

Dedication and Acknowledgments.............................i

Praise iii

Foreword v

Prologue vii

PART I
Chapter 1
A Life Worth Living................................1
Chapter 2
To Hell...3
Chapter 3
Back from Hell....................................7
Chapter 4
Crack Hell..11
Chapter 5
When Hell Freezes Over 15
Chapter 6
Abundant Life Begins 19
Chapter 7
"As Long as There Is Breath in
Your Body, There Is Hope" 23
Chapter 8
Helping Others Practice Empowerment (HOPE) 25
Chapter 9
Mothers In Crisis (MIC) Is Formed 29
Chapter 10
Turning Point International Church (TPIC) Is Born 41

PART II
Chapter 11
The Hurricanes of Life............................49

CHAPTER 12
EVERYTHING THAT CAN BE SHAKEN IS SHAKEN 53
CHAPTER 13
THE NATIONS ARE CALLING.. 61
CHAPTER 14
THE TIDE IS TURNING 63
CHAPTER 15
THROWING BACK THE CATFISH 67
CHAPTER 16
MAKING A LOVE CONNECTION 69
CHAPTER 17
MARRIAGE AND MINISTRY... 75

PART III
CHAPTER 18
IMMERSED IN HOPE 83
CHAPTER 19
SOUTH AFRICAN HOPE TOUR 89
CHAPTER 20
THE EIGHT PEARLS OF WISDOM REVISITED 93

PART IV
CHAPTER 21
RELEASING THE POWER OF HOPE 119
CHAPTER 22
HOPE THOUGHTS AND POEMS OF HOPE 135

ADDENDUM
GLOSSARY 151
ABOUT THE AUTHOR... 155

Dedication and Acknowledgments

I dedicate this book to all those who are leading quiet, desperate lives, wondering if this is all there is. I also dedicate this book to those caring and concerned individuals who want to help others find hope. "May the God of hope fill you with all joy and peace as you trust in him, so that you may overflow with hope by the power of the Holy Spirit" (Romans 15:13, NIV).

I give God all the praise, glory, and honor for bringing me "through many dangers, toils, and snares" by his "amazing grace."

I thank God for my very supportive and loving husband, Richard Lester Kwame Lewis. You continue to fill my life with many unexpected blessings as our love grows. You are truly a gift of hope from the Lord.

I thank God for the Christ Vision Tribe of Mothers In Crisis, the Hope Squad, and the Citizens of Hope. I could not carry out this mandate from God were it not for your continued prayers, encouragement, and support.

I thank God for my spiritual father, Dr. Steven Govender, and his dear wife, Nancy, who consistently provide spiritual covering and support.

I thank God for my daughter, Janar, and my mother, Louise Oates Clark, who majorly influenced my life and helped me to find my way.

Last but not least, I thank the Holy Spirit of the Living God, who is my best friend.

Praise

"I read *As Long as There Is Breath in Your Body, There Is Still Hope*, and two things stand up and out as the Word says they will: the blood of Jesus and the strength of [Pastor Tompkins's] triumphant testimony. To God be the glory! Thank you, Pastor Tompkins, through the Word and the Spirit, for being a breathing example of the love of Jesus and God our Father that consoles us with hope through grace. Excellent book!"

—Cynthia Kimble, MD

"As I read through this book, the Holy Spirit touched the very core of my being, and I shed tears many times as I sensed his presence. Dr. Tompkins has been called by God 'for such a time as this' [Esther 4:14, King James Version, hereafter KJV] to impart faith, hope, and love to many who will allow the Lord to minister to them in this hour, as many face hopelessness. The stories of many whose lives have been transformed will bring great joy and unspeakable glory. As you identify with them, your life will never be the same, in Jesus's name. As you read through this book, get ready to receive all that God has for you."

—Dr. Steven Govender, Restoration and Revival Ministries International

Foreword

We are living in a world and a time in which one of the rarest commodities is hope. Can one manufacture hope? Where does it originate? If it becomes lost, how does one regain it? What are the actual benefits of hope, and even more importantly, what happens when a person sees no ray of hope?

Many people have written books on faith: what faith is, how to obtain strong faith, how to live by faith. But hope, my friend, precedes faith. Faith is a substance, for sure, but it's only "the substance of things *hoped* for" (emphasis added). It then becomes "the evidence of things not seen" (Hebrews 11:1, KJV).

I've traveled around the world for nearly forty years and visited 144 countries, and the one common denominator amongst all people and groups, regardless of their diversity, is hope. It remains the lifeline that keeps people longing for life. Without hope, there is no true quality of life. This is why hope is so vital. This is also why I'm so grateful to this author. In a unique and explicit way, she not only navigates the reader toward obtaining hope but also provides a practical roadmap to regain hope if it's been lost.

As you embrace the very essence of what this book offers you as a reader, you will discover that the author possesses a grace and wisdom that far exceeds literary accuracy. She is beyond a shadow of a doubt not only called but mandated and deputized by the Almighty to rescue those who are in desperate need of hope. She holds a PhD in "hopeology." Her wisdom and compassion leap off the pages of this book and right into the core of your heart—even if you've experienced pain, rejection, betrayal, or just the simple disappointments of life.

This book has the incredible ability to turn your disappointments into divine appointments. As you read it, you will reexamine your perspectives about life and your challenges. You will learn practical ways to obtain hope and tangible ways to share that hope with others who so desperately need it. You will learn how to adopt a lifestyle of hope that will supersede any challenges of life.

Because of the struggle of addiction Dr. Rosalind conquered, she imparts wisdom and the practical applications of hope. She helps you to know that as long as there is breath in you, there's always hope. This book is a must-read. Your life will never be the same.

—Dr. Patricia Bailey, International Missionary,
Master's Touch Ministry (MTM Global)

Prologue

Everyone has a story to tell. *As Long as There Is Breath in Your Body, There Is Still Hope* is my life story of hope.

In my previous book—*As Long as There Is Breath in Your Body, There Is Hope*—I shared some of my experiences from my drug addiction, my recovery, and the founding of the nonprofit organization, Mothers In Crisis (MIC). I also shared eight pearls of wisdom I received from my journey through the hellhole of addiction. In *As Long as There Is Breath in Your Body, There Is Still Hope*, I pick up where the first book left off. Over the fourteen years that have passed since that book was published, I have had to learn how to live clean and sober while facing many incidents that could have zapped me of all hope. Despite those experiences, I am happy to say I am still clean, sober, and full of hope.

This book also explains what happened to MIC after we lost all our grant funding during the economic downturn that hit the United States. As you read, it will become clear that MIC has created a virtual dynasty of hope. I also revisit and upgrade the eight pearls of wisdom to include the additional lessons I learned while traveling around the world to share my story and spread hope. Finally, I share a way of life called the practice of hopeology, which I developed while learning how to receive and release hope.

While one of the main themes of *As Long as There Is Breath in Your Body, There Is Still Hope* is drug and alcohol addiction, the principles of hope in this book can be applied to all life's challenges. I pray that as you read, you will be inspired and filled with hope, no matter what you are facing in your life. I also pray that you will be equipped to share hope with others who are suffering and feel like giving up.

1

A Life Worth Living

Are you breathing?

You're probably thinking, *That's obvious*.

Not so fast. When I ask whether you are breathing, I am referring to whether you are *living*. I'm referring to living in terms of what the Bible teaches about abundant life—not merely existing but truly living and doing it with peace, love, and joy.

It's impossible to live that way when you are addicted to alcohol and drugs. Addiction robs its victims of abundant life and reduces an addicted person to merely existing. I have met thousands of people whose lives were ripped apart by the hellhole of addiction, people reduced to merely existing. I was one of those people. I spent twelve years addicted to various drugs. I started using marijuana when I was twelve years old. My addiction progressed until I was a full-blown crack-cocaine addict by the age of twenty-two. By the grace of God, I was able to turn a hopeless, desperate situation into a place of hope. My journey to hope began at the place of desperation.

Hopeless people are desperate people. Here, then, is the question: What will you do with the desperation? There are many things you can do, but only one thing matters: you need to allow the desperation to lead to brokenness. Why would you choose brokenness? Because brokenness leads to searching for solutions different from the ones you have tried before. That's what happened to me on my journey to hope. I had to try something different and take another path because the path I was on was leading me nowhere but down—fast.

2

To Hell

My pathway to hope through brokenness began when I was nineteen and a sophomore at Florida State University. My daily diet at the time consisted of drugs (including, among others, cocaine and marijuana) and alcohol, and I got high as often as I could. My health was the furthest thing from my mind; I didn't exercise or eat nutritious foods, completely oblivious to the effects my lifestyle had on my body.

Everything fell apart one day during Christmas break in 1982. I remember it as if it were yesterday. My roommate and I were supposed to go to Germany to visit her parents for the holidays. We had the tickets, our passports, and everything else we needed for the trip. Everything, that is, except the drugs.

At the moment it happened, I was alone in our apartment. My roommate had gone out with a friend to try to find some drugs. I was standing in the bathroom, looking in the mirror and talking to myself. That was not something I normally did, but I wasn't used to being alone.

Suddenly it happened: it seemed as if something or someone entered my body. My eyes filled with tears, and my thoughts raced. "Rituals" popped into my mind at an alarming rate—nonsensical cause-and-effect thoughts completely unrelated to reality. I was convinced that God was talking to me. It was like nothing I had ever experienced, even while taking hallucinogenic drugs.

When my roommate returned, she took one look at me and asked me what in the hell had happened to me. I told her I had just had an experience with God. She wanted to know what I had been smoking.

Years later, I realized that hell had happened to me—a thought that had completely eluded me at the time. I am convinced that hell begins in the mind. If it's true that the mind is the battlefield of addiction, I was already desperately losing the war.

Before my roommate and I could leave for Germany, we first had to go to my home in Pensacola, Florida so I could see my mother and family before I left. As it turned out, there would be no Germany—not for me, anyway. While in Pensacola, I completely lost touch with reality and had to be hospitalized. Among other erratic behaviors, I stared at people I didn't know and continued to hear conversations in my head telling me what to do. My mother and stepfather committed me to a psychiatric hospital.

Instead of spending the holidays in Germany with my roommate, I spent them in the mental ward. My medications caused stiff joints, and drool constantly dribbled from the side of my mouth. However, I was convinced there was nothing wrong with *me*. Caught up in paranoid delusions, I thought *everybody else* was the problem—my mother, my roommate, the man walking down the street, *anybody* but me. The doctors were baffled: I had no history of mental illness, and there were no drugs in my system when I was admitted to the hospital. What could be causing my symptoms? During the initial psychosocial interview, the doctors discovered I was an addict, and so they finally determined I was experiencing a flashback because of the "mushroom tea" (a hallucinogen) I had drunk all summer.

For a long time, I was angry about the fact that my roommate had used the same drugs I did but hadn't had a mental breakdown. I couldn't understand why she was able to go to Germany while I was locked up in a psychiatric hospital. That was easy for my roommate to explain, of course: she claimed that while she was strong, I was weak. Part of my anger stemmed from the fact that I believed her—I somehow assumed that had I been strong, I wouldn't have "lost it." But she didn't stop there: she also accused me of faking the breakdown. (As you can well imagine, our friendship did not survive the strain of my illness.)

When I was released from the hospital, I insisted that I be allowed to live with my brother and sister-in-law in Miami. My mother was against that idea, and I should have listened to her. Moving there was one of the worst things I could have done; in that environment, I continued to smoke marijuana and snort cocaine daily. After about a month, I lost touch with reality and began to scream uncontrollably. I was taken to Jackson Memorial Hospital in the back of a police car. While I regained some control during the ride, I started to scream the minute I entered the hospital waiting room. Medical personnel immediately rushed me to a back room, where they strapped me down and cuffed my hands to a bed. I felt like a trapped animal.

That first night, I hallucinated all night long, seeing snakes, screaming loudly, and banging my head against the walls. The next day, the hospital staff put me in a padded, locked room in the back of the hospital so I would not disturb anyone or hurt myself. The only thing in my cell was a bed.

My thoughts were racing, and I felt like a wild animal. I began to crawl around on my hands and knees. I tore the sheets off the bed, threw them across the room, and defecated on the bare mattress. Whenever I was taken from the room, it was in a wheelchair, with one of my hands cuffed to the chair.

I was completely out of control, and I can still remember how totally powerless and helpless I felt. It was as if a two-headed monster had entered my body and driven me out. In retrospect, I believe I was possessed by a demonic spirit. I am reminded of the scriptural account in Luke 8, in which a man possessed by demons was relegated to living in the tombs. After my ordeal in the padded cell, I understand why.

During the next two years, I was admitted to psychiatric hospitals three additional times, but this experience was unquestionably the worst.

3

Back from Hell

When my mother first came to see me at Jackson Memorial Hospital, I didn't even recognize her. I thought she was my sister. I was in such a psychotic state I didn't know my head from my toes for a solid week.

The turning point came when my mother, aunt, sister, and cousins came and prayed for me at the hospital. I was still in such bad condition that hospital personnel had to bring me into the dayroom in a wheelchair; I was strapped to the chair and drooling. My mother asked me if I recognized my family members. Suddenly it was as if a light dawned, and I was able to name each person. I was once again in touch with reality. We joined hands as a family and began to pray.

After that visit, I miraculously gained some sense of control. The demonic spirit controlling me left, and I felt like a human being again. After that day, I was taken from the padded cell and put with the rest of the patients on the ward.

However, I wasn't out of the woods yet. While on the ward, I had to sleep with my shoes under my pillow. If I didn't, I woke up "seeing" other patients wearing my shoes. As I gradually regained full possession of my faculties, I realized where I was and what I'd done—and it wasn't a pretty picture. I felt tremendous shame and guilt. To me the hospital felt like a zoo for human beings. We were treated like animals who had to be forced into submission through restraints and medication. As I became more and more able to think clearly, my mother prepared to take me home with her to Pensacola.

I am so glad I was more in touch with reality at this time because I was able to keep an awful situation from becoming even more terrible. One evening, a male attendant woke me up in the middle of the night and took me to the padded cell where I had spent the first week of my stay. I couldn't imagine why I was being taken there at that hour. I hadn't been hollering or banging my head or being disruptive in any way—I had simply been sleeping.

To my horror, once we were in the cell, the attendant unzipped his pants and tried to make me perform oral sex on him. I kept my mouth tightly closed and shook my head from side to side until he took me back to my room. I thank God this man didn't force me. I didn't tell my family or the hospital staff about what happened because I feared they wouldn't believe me. After all, I had been institutionalized for bizarre behavior.

Once again, the hospital psychiatrists and staff had a hard time ascertaining exactly why I had had a mental breakdown. They eventually attributed it to the drugs I had been taking, and they believed the drug abuse had resulted in a chemical imbalance. When I was eventually discharged and allowed to go home to Pensacola with my mother, the hospital psychiatrist gave her a bottle of pills for me and a prescription for more, saying I would have to take them for the rest of my life. But my mother threw the pills into a big green dumpster on the way out of the hospital and refused to fill the prescription. And I am pleased to say that I haven't had a psychotic episode in the more than thirty-five years since then—because I believe God gave me my mind back!

As a result of these alarming experiences, I was broken to a certain degree. I began to understand that I wasn't invincible. I even decided to make a few changes in my life. However, I still had too much of "me" in me. I believed I had a right to do what I wanted to do whenever I wanted to do it. I did realize I couldn't take certain kinds of drugs (after all, that was what had put me in the hospital twice), but I figured that others were okay.

I would soon learn how wrong I was.

4

Crack Hell

I eventually moved back to Tallahassee to continue attending Florida State University, just as I had told everyone I would. You would think that after my experiences, I would have learned to stay away from drugs and alcohol—but that wasn't the case. I was convinced I needed to avoid only mushroom tea and other hallucinogenic drugs; everything else was fair game. So I continued to smoke marijuana, snort cocaine, and drink alcohol. Only the grace of God kept me from losing my mind again.

In the summer of 1984, freebase cocaine—a "new" drug—hit the streets of Tallahassee, and I was there to meet it. There was nothing new about it; it was nothing more than a different form of an old drug. Freebasing involved cooking cocaine powder with baking soda until it became hard and then smoking it with a pipe. It was the same drug comedian Richard Pryor was smoking when he caught on fire. While freebase cocaine was extremely dangerous, it seemed harmless.

My friends and I freebased for hours because the drug keeps its users from sleeping. On many occasions, I thought I was in heaven. I didn't realize I had made my way back to hell until I was introduced to crack cocaine. All of a sudden, the freebase cocaine came prepackaged and cut (mixed) with God only knows what. It was sold in rock form and was relatively cheap compared to powdered cocaine.

I have never experienced a high as demonic as the crack-cocaine high. It is demanding and consuming, seductive and destructive—all at the same time. When I would smoke the first rock of a hit, I'd experience an instantaneous rush within about eight seconds. I continued to smoke rock after rock, trying to experience that initial rush, but it never came. If I didn't get high, my body ached all over and I couldn't sleep or concentrate for five or six hours after my last hit. Still, the desire for that high drove me to continue using at all costs. People I've known have sold everything in their houses, including the food in the refrigerator, to get another hit.

Crack cocaine was cheap to buy, but the price was high in terms of my self-respect—and more. I got pregnant while exchanging sex for drugs. Once I became clean and sober, I realized that such an exchange was a stupid move, but at the time I was hopelessly addicted and had to have the drug no matter what. Though I carried his child, I don't even remember the man's name.

I tried to stop using drugs while I was pregnant. While I mostly stopped using crack cocaine, I continued to smoke marijuana and occasionally snort powder cocaine. I also smoked cigarettes heavily. Then, during my sixth month of pregnancy, the baby stopped breathing. My doctors had to induce labor, and I experienced all the pain of a natural childbirth, but I never heard my baby cry. She was stillborn. I named her Janadra Elizabeth Tompkins.

Her birth was a sort of wakeup call for me. I began to realize that life was not a joke or one big party. I wasn't laughing; as a matter of fact, I was crying because it hurt like hell. I wrote in my journal, "Why, God? There has to be a reason for going through all of this pain."

Only later in my life did I discover what the reason was, as you will see as my story continues to unfold. During my four psychiatric hospitalizations, I'd learned what it felt like to have a broken mind. The brokenness I experienced at this time was not of the mind but of the heart, and although both were very painful experiences, there was a big difference.

The brokenness of my heart over losing my unborn child was in knowing I could not get her back. She was gone forever. Unfortunately, the brokenness of my spirit was still many life experiences away. I say unfortunately because once my spirit was broken I surrendered totally to God.

5

When Hell Freezes Over

You've heard the saying "There's no place like home." That seemed particularly true for me, so after Janadra's birth, I went to stay with my mother and stepfather. I was quite depressed. All I did was watch television, eat, and think long and hard about my life as I recuperated from the loss of my baby.

My mother and stepfather lived near the Pensacola Bay, and every day I went to a park on the water called Bayview. I sat and looked out at the water, trying to imagine where I would be in five years. I saw nothing but darkness. I knew I had to do something or I would die on the vine, so I once again decided to go back to Tallahassee to continue my education.

I returned to Florida State University determined to change my life, but I wasn't completely through with marijuana. I deceived myself into believing marijuana wasn't a problem, telling myself it was just an herb grown by nature. Besides, my troubles had started only when I had used other drugs. I even had an image of myself smoking a joint as a grandmother while sitting in a rocking chair on the back porch. Frankly, I had no intentions of giving up weed.

During my coursework, I got a job in the mall doing surveys for a marketing company. I was good at it, and I worked all day, walking around the mall to get people to participate. On one occasion, I was trying to get respondents who fit a certain profile for a malt-liquor survey. In this case, the company was looking for young black men. So was I, though not for the same reason.

As I searched, I spotted a tall, milk-chocolate-colored young man sitting as though he were just killing time. I approached him and asked if he drank malt liquor and if he would like to participate in a survey. He said he did drink malt liquor—and that he would participate in the survey if I gave him my name and telephone number. Needless to say, I did, and we began to talk. The man (whom I'll call Sam) explained that he was in the navy and stationed in Jacksonville, but he and his friends had only been driving through Gadsden County when his car broke down. Gadsden County is very rural, and since there weren't any mechanics available at that time, the car had been towed to Tallahassee. Sam rode with the tow-truck driver and was waiting for his friends to come and pick him up. They had decided to go to their destination so it wouldn't be until much later that night. Since I lived close to the mall, I asked if he would like to come to my apartment and wait for them. He eagerly agreed. The rest is history.

Sam began coming to see me as often as he could, and I fell in love with him. I thought I had finally found someone with whom I could live happily ever after. For the first time in a very long time, drugs were not the center of my life. I was still smoking marijuana, but I really was trying to do the right thing and turn my life around, so I refused to have sex with Sam. He respected that for the most part, but we still hugged and kissed and even slept in the same bed.

Then, in the wee hours of one morning, I woke up in the act of making love and gave in to a temptation that was much too close to resist. Over the course of our relationship, which lasted about a year, we made love only that one time, but that was all it took. Sam was out to sea when I found out I was pregnant. I really didn't want to be pregnant, but I was so naïve I thought once Sam found out, we would get married.

That didn't happen.

He never called or came back. I wrote to him and even called him to tell him about my pregnancy. When we spoke, Sam told me he was already married and he didn't know why "all these things" were happening to him. I said I didn't know what was happening to him, but I knew what was happening to me, and I asked him what he planned to do about it. He said he would do what he could to take care of the baby. That was the last time I ever heard from him.

I was devastated. I didn't know what to do. I talked to my boss at the marketing firm, and she told me to continue to work. I did, and for the first time in twelve long years, I stopped smoking marijuana. I actually stopped. It was hard. On some days, after walking around the mall all day and finally going home to an empty apartment, I simply cried, despairing unto death.

I began to pray and read my Bible. I mainly asked God to send my boyfriend back because my heart was broken. I also asked the Lord for a healthy baby. I didn't want to go through another stillbirth, as I had with Janadra Elizabeth, so I stopped using drugs, alcohol, and cigarettes altogether.

I made it through the nine months and gave birth to a healthy baby girl. I named her Janar Shenale Tompkins. It was then that I realized I had to be responsible for someone other than myself, and I decided to breastfeed my baby. I knew I couldn't use drugs while breastfeeding because the drugs would get into the baby's system through my milk.

I was determined to remain drug free, but it wasn't easy once my old friends started to come back around. On one occasion, I took Janar to visit a neighbor with whom I used to smoke marijuana. We were all sitting around talking about my baby when my friends fired up a joint and began passing it around. When it came to me, I was faced with a major decision. I knew if I took a hit of that joint, I would start using regularly again. Everything in me wanted to taste the weed to which I had grown accustomed for twelve years. But when the joint came to me, Janar suddenly began to cry, waking me out of the trancelike state into which I had slipped. I took my baby and left. I never visited that neighbor again.

After I had lost my mind on four different occasions, lost my self-respect, conceived a child while on crack cocaine, and ultimately lost the man I loved, my spirit was finally broken. I felt like a wild stallion that was finally tamed. I began to search for answers from that brokenness and sought help to change my life. I had reached the end of my rope; I didn't know where to go, what to do, or whom to call.

I decided to call on Jesus. I surrendered my will to God, accepted Jesus as my Savior, and said to the Lord, "I give up. I will do whatever you want me to do." After that, my journey of hope expanded exponentially, and I began to reach out to others who needed help and hope.

6

Abundant Life Begins

In John 10:10 (ESV), the Lord says, "The thief comes only to steal and kill and destroy. I came that they may have life and have it abundantly." This abundant life in Christ Jesus began for me once I quit using drugs and alcohol and allowed the Lord to lead and guide me.

After six long years of ups and downs, I finally graduated from Florida State University with a bachelor's degree in social work. I was still working in the mall, doing surveys and marketing work in the field; it was a decent job, but the pay wasn't great, and there was no room for advancement. When Janar was six months old, I decided it was time to use my degree to get a better job that would bring in a better income. As a single parent with no child support, I really needed it. When I was unable to find Sam for potential financial help, I decided to take care of Janar myself, without government assistance.

I had been clean only one year, but the first job I got in my field of expertise was working at a residential drug-treatment program as a mental-health technician on the midnight shift, where I made only $4.75 an hour. It wasn't exactly what I had had in mind, but I felt it would give me the experience I needed to qualify me for other jobs in social work. I mainly babysat the clients at night and then went home to take care of Janar during the day.

It was a time of great transition in my life, and it wasn't easy. It seemed as though I never slept. I was happy, though, because I had my baby girl and I was still drug free. I also began to get a taste of what it felt like to help someone else. Before having Janar, I had been very selfish: it was all about me and what I wanted. Now I was beginning to think about others. It had started with Janar and now extended to the people who were in treatment, especially the women. I could identify with them because I had gone through much of the same thing.

After working as a mental-health technician for almost a year, I was promoted to the newly formed position of intervention specialist. It was a match made in heaven. The state of Florida was providing funding for intervention specialists across the state to deal with the problem of pregnant women using drugs (primarily crack cocaine) and having what people were calling "crack babies." These were babies who were experiencing extreme withdrawal because of the crack-cocaine used by their mothers during pregnancy. Part of my responsibilities included using referrals from various organizations in Leon and Gadsden Counties, such as health departments, hospitals, the Department of Health and Rehabilitative Services (HRS), which was the state of Florida's child protection agency, and various nonprofit agencies—to identify women who needed treatment.

Many of the women with whom I worked were pregnant and using crack cocaine; some had just given birth to babies who had cocaine in their system. As I looked into the eyes of these women, I often saw myself staring back at me. I remembered what hopelessness and despair felt like. I remembered not knowing my head from my toes, and I desperately wanted to help these women with their recovery. Unfortunately, there was not much in the way of treatment available for pregnant and parenting women who were using drugs, especially in rural communities.

In an attempt to provide treatment, I began facilitating drug-education support-group meetings at a health department in Gadsden County and a neighborhood community center in Leon County. I used an agency van to pick up the women from their homes and bring them to the meetings. As I helped them, I learned many things that helped me understand why I had gone through so much in my own life. I'd needed those experiences to help me to become nonjudgmental and to persevere with love and compassion through some tremendously emotional situations.

I'll never forget the time I went to pick up a young lady I'll call Cecilia from a drug-infested housing project in Havana, Florida. I had to literally dodge bullets to get to her apartment—local police officers were exchanging fire with a drug dealer they were trying to apprehend. Then Cecilia got into the van with her four children, and one of my other passengers called my attention to something not right about Cecilia. I confronted Cecilia and asked that she open her tightly balled fist. When she did, there in her hand was a "stem" (homemade pipe), still smoking hot from her just having taken a hit.

My first instinct was to demand that Cecilia get out of the van. However, as I looked at her disheveled hair and clothes and children, who were all gazing back at me with sad eyes, I was moved with compassion. I took the stem, told Cecilia and her children to sit down, and closed the door. That day, I drove to the meeting in tears. Unfortunately, Cecilia never quit using, and her children were eventually removed from her custody.

I learned a great deal from working with these women. Thankfully, one of the greatest lessons I learned early on is that everyone is responsible for his or her own recovery. No matter how much I may have wanted the women to get clean, how much their families wanted them to get clean, or how much the government wanted them to get clean, *they* had to want to be clean and sober.

I believe that abundant life consists of knowing your purpose and destiny in life as it unfolds and choosing to live according to God's will. Abundant life is a choice. You choose whether you will receive the gift of salvation. I chose life through recovery from drugs and alcohol, and I have continued to choose life in Christ one day at a time for more than thirty years. Before, I was merely existing; now I am truly living.

7

"As Long as There Is Breath in Your Body, There Is Hope"

Many evenings, after working in the field all day and picking up Janar from day care, I went home mentally, emotionally, and physically drained. I was often discouraged because it seemed the women I worked with were not getting and staying clean. After attending great support-group meetings, these women went back home into drug-ridden communities, where many of them continued to smoke crack.

I vividly remember one night that changed my life and my work forever. I'd finally made it home after a long and emotionally taxing day of working with the women. I fed Janar, put her to bed, and sat in the dark in the small living room of my duplex, crying as I thought about the day's events.

I was running a support group in Tallahassee at the time, and one of the attendees (whom I'll call Alaina) had left her purse in the van that day. She lived in a rural town called Quincy, so one of the attendees from Tallahassee (whom I'll call Gerri) and I drove out to return the purse. When we got to Alaina's house, her sister told us Alaina had gone around the corner. I drove there, and when Alaina spotted me, she looked as though she had seen a ghost.

She walked over to the van, and as she spoke to me, I noticed that her mouth was twitching sideways. I had never seen this before, and I thought she might be having a stroke. Gerri leaned over and whispered that Alaina must have just taken a hit of crack cocaine.

I asked Alaina if she would like a ride home. With her mouth twitching so much I could hardly understand what she was saying, she responded, "No, but thanks for bringing me my purse." I got out of the van and asked Alaina to please come with us so she could get help, and offered to take her to a detox facility in Tallahassee. She responded, "No, just give me my purse." I reluctantly handed her the purse, hugged her, and got back in the van. Gerri and I prayed for her as we traveled back to Tallahassee. (Many years later, I learned that Alaina was eventually shot and killed by an abusive boyfriend.)

As I sat in my dark living room that night, crying and praying, I knew I could not continue this much longer. It was taking a toll on me, and I was feeling hopeless again for the first time in many years. Suddenly, I heard a still, small voice inside me saying, "Rosalind, the ladies are in My hands, just as you are. Cast them upon Me and leave them there, and remember, *as long as there is breath in their bodies, there is hope.* Don't give up on them, just as I didn't give up on you."

I realized that the message had come from the Lord, and I never let go of that thought. Afterward, whenever I started to feel discouraged, I repeated a version of this phrase to myself: "As long as there is breath in your body, there is hope." I even trademarked this statement with the US Patent Office and used it in the public-service announcements I wrote and produced for more than ten years. Over the years, many women have told me how mightily they have been affected by this powerful idea.

8

Helping Others Practice Empowerment (HOPE)

After receiving "As long as there is breath in your body, there is hope," I knew that there was hope as long as people were alive and that I needed to empower them to keep living. From then on, empowerment became a part of what I instilled in the women with whom I worked. For me, empowerment was illustrated in the saying "If you give a man a fish, he will eat for a day, but if you teach him how to fish, he will eat for life."

Empower means "to [give] power or authority; to enable or permit." The women with whom I worked needed to be given the power to get and stay clean. They desperately needed tools to remain clean and sober no matter what was going on in their environment. I believe that power is packaged in hope. To give hope is to give power.

When I shared my personal story and demonstrated that recovery was possible and that there was a way out, many of the women grabbed ahold of the "rope" of hope I offered them. Unlike some methods of helping addicts, I didn't agree with the idea of constantly declaring that one was an addict or resolving oneself to powerlessness. I did understand that the women needed to first admit they had a problem in order to break through the denial. However, after that, they needed to be empowered to believe they didn't have to remain powerless addicts. That process of empowerment often included meeting needs for education, job skills, parenting skills, drug and alcohol counseling, housing assistance, love, support, encouragement, and hope. I also knew from my own experience that the key to my ability to stay clean was my personal relationship with the Lord Jesus Christ.

After four years of working with "my women," I became intimately aware of what was available in the state of Florida and throughout the United States for pregnant women who were addicted to drugs and alcohol. It wasn't a pretty picture. The treatment programs were primarily based on a model of confrontation that centered on the prototype of the white male alcoholic. Many programs utilized methods that assumed (often incorrectly) the women had little or no concern for the well-being of their unborn babies. For example, women were often told, "You aren't thinking about your baby," because they were on the streets. As a result, many women were leaving programs without having successful outcomes. I went to many meetings where client treatment plans were being discussed and professionals asked, "What is wrong with these women?" In response, I began to ask, "What is wrong with these treatment programs?"

During the late 1980s and early 1990s, a few counties in Florida began prosecuting women who were using drugs while pregnant. The problem was that even though some of the women were sentenced to treatment programs, there were often no treatment programs available in their areas. Therefore, these women had to stay in jail until they gave birth, this punitive response deterring many women from seeking help.

I became an expert in this field while working for the private, nonprofit treatment center Apalachee Center. The center received a federal grant for a project called Keeping Mothers off Drugs (KMOD), and I was promoted to clinical coordinator of this project. In that position, I attended substance-abuse-treatment training conferences for professionals working with women, infants, and children in some of the best treatment programs in the nation. I traveled to Chicago, Illinois; Washington,

DC; and St. Petersburg, Florida, among other places. I even met Mother Clara Hale, who founded the Hale House in Harlem, New York, in 1969 when she started taking in babies born with drug addictions and AIDS. I also participated in panel discussions and gave presentations at conferences, sharing my personal story of addiction and recovery and my experiences working with female addicts.

I'll never forget my experience in April 1991, when I traveled to Columbia, South Carolina, to speak as part of a team of experts from Tallahassee. The team consisted of a public-health nurse, a state social worker, and me as an intervention specialist from the nonprofit sector. We had been asked to share how we worked together to help women who were using while pregnant to get off drugs and have healthy babies.

I woke up early on the morning of the panel discussion and took a walk. I ended up getting lost. I finally made it back to the large hotel room in which I was staying. It was a suite apartment with two full bedrooms that could have housed another guest quite comfortably. It was the first time I had ever stayed in a suite that size alone. When I returned to my room, it was as I sat quietly and wrote my thoughts in my journal that I felt inspired to start MIC. I wrote that I was to create a national networking ministry to help women overcome addiction.

I did not know it then, but God had given me my life's work. It was through MIC that I learned what true empowerment looks like. Empowerment happens when a person embraces the power available through a personal relationship with the Lord Jesus Christ. From that place, he empowers you by the Holy Spirit to do amazing things, because, as it says in the scriptures, "I can do all things through Christ who gives me strength" (Philippians 4:13, Berean Study Bible).

9

Mothers In Crisis (MIC) Is Formed

While still working at the Apalachee Center for Human Services, I organized and hosted a community event featuring a panel discussion much like the one on which I had participated in Columbia. As part of this discussion, however, I also organized a panel of the women with whom I worked and asked them to share their personal experiences with addiction. Most importantly, I asked them to share their perspective about their needs.

It was the first time anything like that had been done in our area. The prior panel discussions had always been *about* the women who needed help, but none had included these women at the table. I believed the women had to have a voice and be heard as active participants in their treatment plan if they were to truly be empowered. I called the panel discussion "Mothers In Crisis."

This discussion was not only successful, it was groundbreaking. It took place in the late 1980s, in the era of anonymity, before reality television. Today, we don't even blink when people go on television and talk about their addictions and dysfunctional lives, but American culture was very different at that time. One of the panel participants stole the show as she poignantly articulated her experiences. She described how many times she had attempted to stop using drugs and pointed out that there were no drug-treatment programs available for parenting women. After the panel discussion, she entered an inpatient drug-treatment program for women because her voice had finally been heard.

Staff from the Women's Intervention Services and Education (WISE) program in Pensacola, Florida, also attended the panel discussion. They were so impressed with the work I was doing the supervisor recruited me for a coordinator position in the WISE program. I decided to take the job because my mother and family still lived in Pensacola. I was finding single parenting to be somewhat difficult, and I looked forward to receiving help from my family.

While in Pensacola, I informally started Mothers In Crisis National Networking Ministry with the local group of women with whom I was working. I briefly facilitated MIC support-group meetings in both Pensacola and Tallahassee. However, things did not turn out well for me in Pensacola. I did not have the autonomy at the WISE program that I had had at the Apalachee Center. I felt controlled by my supervisor, and I became so depressed I started repeatedly getting sick with cold and flu viruses. I also missed Tallahassee tremendously, and I got tired of traveling back and forth on the weekends, so I eventually resigned from the WISE program and moved back to Tallahassee to officially establish MIC.

While living in Pensacola, I regularly attended New Covenant Christian Church. Though I was quite busy working at WISE and starting MIC (all while being a single parent), I was lonely and still hurting from what had happened with Sam. Things were going well at church until one Sunday when a guest speaker known as a prophetess ministered in the pastor's absence. She shared an inspiring message and then had an altar call for those who wanted prayer. I went to the altar for prayer about all the problems I was having at WISE as well as my feelings of hurt and loneliness. When the prophetess was ready to pray for me, she called a young man (whom I'll call Robert) out of the audience and asked him to come to the altar too. She put our hands together and began to prophesy about our marriage. I was dumbfounded; my mouth dropped wide open. I didn't know what to think.

When the pastor returned and heard about what had happened, he warned me about jumping into a relationship based on prophecy. I thanked him and told him I would put the prophecy in the parking lot—in other words, I would not act on it.

Eventually, however, I took the prophecy out of the parking lot, and Robert and I started dating. It seemed to be going well, although I kept hearing rumors from the women in my support group that Robert was still using drugs. They said things such as, "How can she tell us to quit using while her man is still getting high?" I even had dreams about Robert using crack, but he always denied it. They say love is blind. If that is true, I was blind as a bat, because I convinced myself I was in love and that Robert and I would be okay despite my dreams, which I am now convinced were given to me as a warning.

Robert and I set a wedding date and planned to move back to Tallahassee after we got married, but God had other plans. Two weeks before the wedding, Robert went on a two-day drug binge. I called him at his apartment and went to his workplace, but no one knew where he was. When he finally came by my apartment late one night, I confronted him. I asked him where he had been, and he started to make up a lie. I then told him to tell the truth or leave. Robert confessed to using crack cocaine again and admitted he had been using periodically during the year we had dated.

I was crushed. Feeling like a big fool, I cried and cried. After praying about it, I called the wedding off. We did both move from Pensacola to Tallahassee, and he even attended the same church I did, but I could not trust him again. The relationship was over, and he eventually moved back to his hometown of Atlanta, Georgia.

Once that relationship drama ended, I started having MIC support-group meetings in my two-bedroom duplex. I knew transportation had to be provided for the program to be successful, so we picked the women up in our cars. Childcare was another barrier, so we provided babysitting services for the mothers who needed to bring their children. We often had more children than mothers because some of the women had five or six children who were all under the age of seven.

When I started MIC, Janar was only three years old, and I had four years clean and sober under my belt. Though I remained drug free, I knew I needed additional support in order to stay that way. I was attending church, but I needed more specific help for issues related to drug and alcohol addiction and the other things I had been through. However, I could not relate to the Narcotics Anonymous support groups available in my area at the time. They discouraged participants from expressing religious perspectives about their recoveries, encouraging everyone to use the term *higher power* rather than *God*. Effectively, *God* could be the group, a tree, or whatever. As a black woman whose roots were firmly planted in the soil of the African Methodist Episcopal Church, which I had grown up attending, I could not reduce my relationship with Jesus to experiences with a "higher power." I simply didn't fit in, in these groups.

My motivation for starting MIC initially was to ensure that I could continue to live a drug-free life. I needed the support. I received it through creating a model of intervention and support that was specific to my gender, spirituality, and culture. After I started MIC, I truly started living; my need and desire for drugs completely vanished, and I immersed myself in doing the will of God. I always say MIC works because it has kept me clean and sober for more than thirty years.

In 1993, two years after starting MIC, I attended a weeklong intensive training at the Caspar Treatment Program for Women in Boston, Massachusetts. It was there that I learned about the relational model of intervention. Its basis was the premise that women were primarily relationship oriented and that addiction caused a major disconnect in the relationships women had with their families, their significant others, and especially their children. The whole focus of intervention using the relational model was to help women bridge those gaps and create healthy relationships. Programs using this model reported that the participants flourished and had successful outcomes. When I presented this model to the support team of Mothers In Crisis, we decided to utilize that model in MIC support services.

Although MIC received 501(c)(3) designation as a nonprofit federally tax-exempt organization, and though I wrote and managed several grant-funded programs from 1993 through 2007, MIC did not start out as a grant-funded program, and the officers of Mothers In Crisis vowed to continue with or without grant support. Over the years, I have learned to value that principle—I have worked in this field long enough to see that when grant money ends, programs often end too.

MIC continues to be primarily a volunteer-driven organization that depends on God and volunteers like Millie Poulos, Nettie Walker Palmore, Juanita Thompson, and Sharon Durham. These women's stories and journeys reflect the experiences of many of the people we have helped, so I will briefly share those stories here.

MILLIE'S STORY

Born in Bronx, New York, Millie eventually moved to Long Island, New York, to live with her sister, Martha, and Martha's husband. Martha adopted Millie when their mother was no longer able to care for Millie because of mental illness. Still, things were great for Millie until she turned twelve, at which time she was exposed to a lot of partying, drinking, and cigarette smoking at home. She remembers, "When everyone passed out from drinking, I sampled the alcohol." That was the beginning of her addiction.

Millie met her first husband, Michael, at a tenth-grade dance. She says, "It was love at first sight." They started seeing each other, and Millie became pregnant with their daughter. A couple years later, Millie and Michael got married. Michael joined the army and was stationed at Fort Bragg in Savannah, Georgia.

Then the trouble began. "I went back to New York to visit my mom, and after a week of not hearing from Michael, I called the base," Millie recalls. "The officer who answered the telephone told me, 'I am sorry, Mrs. Figueroa, but Michael Anthony Figueroa has gone AWOL.' Eventually I divorced Michael, and my daughter and I moved on."

A few years later, Millie met her second husband, rhythm guitarist James Alexander Poulos, when she auditioned to be lead singer in a rock-and-roll band. By then, Millie was a full-blown addict, and both she and James used alcohol and crack cocaine. They also dealt drugs and lived the correspondingly chaotic life. Through all the using, dealing, and partying, Millie somehow maintained a job at a major university.

"I eventually got sick and tired of being sick and tired," Millie says, "when my oldest daughter ran away because of the craziness that was going on and was placed in a Florida Baptist children's home. I finally repented and surrendered all to the Lord Jesus Christ, and everything started falling into place." Millie's daughter returned home, and Millie remembers, "The Lord took the taste for crack cocaine out of my mouth. I stopped smoking crack, cigarettes, and weed and drinking alcohol. I finally realized that there is no high like the Most High God."

I met Millie when she was five years clean. Of that time she remembers, "I met Dr. Rosalind Tompkins's melodious voice over the radio airwaves. She had a show called *Mothers In Crisis, Mothers In Christ.* She got my attention with her positive message and soothing voice. When I called MIC, Dr. Tompkins invited me to a meeting, and we have been making history ever since." That was more than two decades ago, and Millie is now a volunteer with the Hope Squad of MIC.

NETTIE'S STORY

Nettie Walker Palmore reflects, "Growing up was rough, because although my mother did the best she could, we lived in a poverty-stricken, rat-infested home that was later condemned."

Nettie took her first drink of alcohol when she was fifteen. At sixteen, she met her first boyfriend, dropped out of school, and moved in with him. "He was physically and verbally abusive, and I drank alcohol until I passed out to numb the pain," she recalls.

After eight years of that abusive relationship, Nettie's boyfriend went to prison. During his incarceration, Nettie met another man. On their first date, they had sex, and she conceived. "I drank alcohol throughout my pregnancy, and I received no prenatal care," Nettie remembers. "I went into labor at seven months. During labor, I slipped into a coma for three days. While in that coma, I delivered a three-pound, seven-and-a-half-ounce baby boy."

Not long after her son was born, Nettie married a man she had met while hanging out on the streets. They had a daughter, and her drinking got worse. She also started smoking crack cocaine. "I became addicted from the first hit," she says. "I would lock myself up in the bathroom late at night to smoke crack. One night as I was smoking, my husband kicked the door in. He cussed me out and beat me."

Following that incident, the Florida Department of Children and Families came to investigate. They found the house and the children intact, but Nettie's drug test came back positive for cocaine. Nettie was told she had to get treatment or lose custody of her children, so she tried outpatient treatment. It didn't work for her, and she continued to use drugs.

Nettie eventually went into an inpatient treatment program and did well, but she left the program early. She started using again, and this time it was worse. "Hope finally came into my life when I heard someone giving testimony of being free from drugs," she says. "I was in my apartment getting high, and I heard a voice outside my window say, 'As long as there is breath in your body, there is hope.' I hid my crack pipe under my bed and ran out of my apartment to see who it was. That's when I met Dr. Rosalind Tompkins."

As it turned out, Nettie had overheard me sharing my story of addiction and recovery during an outdoor church service in her neighborhood. Nettie joined MIC and got clean and sober. That was more than two decades ago, and like Millie, Nettie is now a volunteer with the Hope Squad of MIC.

JUANITA'S STORY

Juanita Thompson was born in Quincy, Florida, a rural community outside Tallahassee, and was reared by her grandparents. After finishing high school, she met a young man, got married, and had a baby girl named Porshala. When Porshala turned six months old, she was diagnosed with sickle cell anemia—and that's when Juanita took her first hit of crack cocaine with her husband.

"Because of the sickle cell anemia, we took many trips back and forth to the hospital," Juanita explains. "It was a battle for many years—seeing Porshala suffering, bound to a hospital bed with tubes connected to her little body. She had to have blood transfusions on several occasions, and I had to listen to her screaming because she was in so much pain."

It was hard dealing with a sick baby, and Juanita and her husband coped by turning to drugs and alcohol. As a mother watching her daughter suffer, Juanita could do nothing to ease Porshala's pain, so she continued to smoke crack to deal with the helplessness she felt.

Juanita and her husband appeared to be doing well in their vocations, but their personal lives were spinning out of control, and they eventually got a divorce. Juanita and Porshala moved to Tallahassee. During her teenage years, Porshala had to have her gall bladder and spleen removed, and she couldn't go to school consistently because of frequent hospitalizations. At one point, Juanita tried to homeschool her, but that lasted only a season.

Juanita eventually got involved in another relationship that resulted in a son named Anthony. However, that relationship also ended badly, as Juanita continued to use drugs. Juanita remembers, "On several occasions when I was getting high, I saw MIC public-service announcements on television that always ended with 'As long as there is breath in your body, there is hope.' Even though I continued to get high when the commercials ended, I now realize that a seed of hope was planted in my heart—because when I was ready, I went looking for MIC."

Juanita remembers, "After using drugs all those years, I began to get very paranoid every time I used crack; I felt like I was on fire. I asked others around me if I was on fire, and they assured me I wasn't, but I jumped up to find a mirror—and when I looked in it, I saw smoke in my hair. My eyes also looked like a fiery furnace. On one occasion, I had plaits in my hair. When I saw what looked like fire in my hair, I cut them all out. Something had to change!"

That change finally came for Juanita one night. "It started as I was traveling back home from Quincy after using drugs all night," she remembers. "I looked up at the sky, and the closer I got to home, the more different the sky looked. Porshala always waited up for me to arrive. That night was no different. When I walked inside, I told Porshala, 'This is the last time.' She responded, 'I've heard it all before.'

"I went into my bedroom and went to sleep. When I woke up the next morning, everything was new. God had delivered me in my sleep! I woke up totally changed after being addicted to drugs and alcohol for twenty years. I no longer wanted or desired the drugs or alcohol."

Shortly after that, Juanita came to MIC. She started attending support-group meetings and Turning Point International Church, the chapel outreach ministry of MIC (see chapter 10). She testifies, "They truly supported me in my recovery with great counseling, teaching, and tools to use to stay clean and sober." That was more than a decade ago, and Juanita is now a volunteer with the Hope Squad.

Porshala, who joined Turning Point International with Juanita, continued to suffer with sickle cell anemia. Some of her sickle-cell crises required hospitalizations, and on several occasions, she left church service and went directly to the hospital. Porshala explains, "A sickle cell crisis feels like being hit with a hammer nonstop." There were times when Porshala couldn't walk because of the pain from a crisis, and Juanita had to bathe her.

Several years after Juanita became clean and sober, Porshala started attending adult- and community-education classes to get her GED. The frequent trips to the hospital stopped, and while sickle cell anemia still afflicts her body, Porshala is doing much better at managing her life and her disease.

SHARON'S STORY

Sharon Durham is a veteran who served in Operation Desert Storm and was later honorably discharged from the military. She grew up in a single-parent home with her mother and brother. Sharon and her brother were very close, and almost every weekend, they stayed with their maternal grandparents, where they attended church every Sunday. Sharon explains, "I spent almost the entire summer with my grandparents, and my brother went to St. Petersburg and visited his dad the entire summer."

Sharon's father came to visit her for only a couple hours every now and then, and when he did, she was always extremely excited to see him. She recalls, "He made all kinds of promises that he would be back the next day and take me shopping, and I believed him every time. Sometimes he came on a Sunday and told me, 'When you get out of school tomorrow, come to your grandmother's house.' I ran almost all the way to her house—just to be told he had gone back to Orlando. No matter how many times he came to town and told me things like that, I always believed him."

At the age of nineteen, Sharon married David Durham, the love of her life, and her dad gave her away at the wedding. After that, they occasionally kept in touch with each other. Still, Sharon says, "My anger and rejection issues grew, and Dr. Rosalind Tompkins counseled me about forgiveness. Through her counseling, I was able to forgive my dad, and I realized that people can't give you what they don't have. The forgiveness came when I realized we can't change the past and that as long as I continued to dwell on how my dad had not been there for me when I was a child, I would not be able to move forward in life." Once Sharon allowed God to heal her, she was able to let all the hurt and pain go. She says, "Now my relationship with my dad is great; we talk every week, we visit, and we have a close father-daughter relationship with mutual love and respect."

Sharon has suffered a lot of loss, including the deaths of her grandmother, aunt, and best friend. Three years ago, her cousin Tracey was killed in a tragic accident, which badly injured Sharon's emotional well-being. She explains, "Tracey's death greatly affected me because we were very close. I never realized how much I was hurting until he passed. In my mind, I thought I had it all together, mainly because I attended church every time the doors opened."

But Sharon *didn't* have it all together. She wore a mask and put on a happy "church face," saying all the right things around others while hoping no one could see the real Sharon. "I was pretending to be happy when I was not," she says. "I overanalyzed what others thought of me, and I was clingy in my friendships. I also harbored and stuffed down my feelings of fear. Sometimes I drank alcohol to ease my pain, but I realize now that drinking only made things worse because I had already been diagnosed with post-traumatic stress disorder from my time in the military."

In June 2017, everything changed. "I could no longer pretend anymore," Sharon remembers. "I became broken, and I left MIC and the church. I just left and was determined to never come back, but as I grew closer to God, I realized I had to go back and make things right."

In April 2018, Sharon emailed me and set up a meeting to ask forgiveness for how she had departed. Sharon explains, "If I could describe how I left, it would be like coming home after thirty-eight years of marriage and finding that my husband had left without a trace. I had to go because God had to get my attention, and he did. God helped me take off the masks through prayer, fasting, and reading his Word daily. I realized I couldn't do this on my own, so I went to Christian counseling. I am now healing one day at a time as I attend hope coaching with Dr. Rosalind Tompkins. I'm also back at Turning Point International Church and volunteering with MIC. I know that as long as I trust in God, there is hope!"

10

Turning Point International Church (TPIC) Is Born

MIC was a faith-based organization before it was acceptable or popular to be so, and it has taken a lot of faith to continue year after year. Our faith is what has kept us going during the lean and mean times. The last time we counted, in 2008, MIC had helped more than ten thousand families live drug- and alcohol-free lives. Since then, we have affected thousands more—and one of the ways we continue to reach out to families is through Turning Point International Church (TPIC), the chapel outreach ministry of MIC. Three of the members of MIC joined me to start TPIC in July 1998.

I was first ordained a minister in 1996 by my former pastor, Tom Cabell, at Christian Victory Fellowship Church, a nondenominational charismatic church Janar and I attended in Tallahassee. At the time, I was facilitating support-group meetings for the women of MIC, and I also had a prison outreach, in which a team and I ministered weekly to the women at Gadsden Correctional Institution. I was happy to finally be ordained because I was already ministering, but I did not want to be a pastor. I ran hard from that call, but God had his way in the end.

My friends from MIC and I started TPIC in a storefront on Holton Street in a drug-infested, high-crime neighborhood on the Southside of Tallahassee. The MIC house was also located on the Southside. Both were strategically placed amid quite a few crack houses. I felt like a missionary who had been called to the Southside because I lived, ministered, and worked there.

TPIC remained in that location for four years. On several occasions, we literally opened the doors, turned the speakers outward, and ministered to the prostitutes and drug addicts walking the streets outside our building. Many told me they could hear us several blocks away, but the police didn't bother us because they knew we were helping clean up the neighborhood. Women came off the streets and into the chapel, throwing away their drugs and joining MIC.

One of those women was Barbara. She came into the service one night asking for prayer, and we prayed for her. She had been out using crack for weeks, and she was exhausted and dirty. After services, we took her home to her family members, who were glad to see her and welcomed her back. She joined MIC, started attending the weekly support-group meetings, and stopped using drugs. She was one of the sweetest and kindest people I have ever met.

When Barbara joined TPIC, she began to do all she could to help others and help the ministry to grow. She became a deaconess at TPIC and expressed her fervent desire to be used by God. Sadly, she eventually passed away from cancer, but she left her mark as one of the beautiful souls we were honored to help on their journey of hope.

In 2001, I moved my mother, Louise Oates Clark, from Pensacola to live with me in Tallahassee. That same year, the horrendous September 11 terrorist attacks took place in the United States. I will never forget that day. I was at home watching Judge Marilyn Milian of *The People's Court* while getting ready to go to the MIC house. Suddenly a news report interrupted programming, showing footage of airplanes flying into the World Trade Center in New York City. I ran into the living room, where my mother was watching the same thing on television. We were both horrified and saddened.

I went to the MIC house and picked up everyone who was there. We went to TPIC and prayed. I could not stop thinking about the images of people on fire jumping from burning buildings as thousands lost their lives. The wind of change blew hard through America as we entered the world stage of terrorism. For a time after that, there were signs on homes and businesses everywhere that read, "God Bless America."

A year later, TPIC moved from inner-city Tallahassee to the outskirts of Leon County, where we had purchased a church building on an acre of land on State Road 20. Even though we provided transportation, many of the members who had attended TPIC on Holton Street did not come to our new location. Many said it was too far from the community they were used to. However, there were some who did come—women like Daphne Nelson.

DAPHNE'S STORY

Daphne began drinking alcohol when she was ten and using drugs when she was fourteen. As she watched her sister regularly party, Daphne began to sneak a drink here and there. Eventually, drugs and alcohol took over her life.

Years later, as Daphne continued down a self-destructive path, she was raped. While incarcerated for driving under the influence, she found out she was six months pregnant. Though Daphne continued to use drugs heavily while pregnant, her baby girl—Tamdalalia, or Tam—was born healthy.

Daphne was shaken into the reality of what she had done when she was not allowed to take Tam home from the hospital. "I could not believe that because of my lifestyle, this was happening to me," she remembers. "When I first laid eyes on Tam in the delivery room, it was like a light bulb had come on. I knew it was a sign from God that I had to be a mother and get my act together. It was painful having to spend even one day without my brand-new baby girl."

Daphne was allowed only supervised visits with Tam, who was placed in the custody of a family member after being released from the hospital. Daphne was given a case plan by the Department of Children and Families and told she had to get clean and sober before she could regain custody of Tam. Daphne says, "I started scrambling to find the proper help. I was familiar with MIC because I had seen how they helped another woman I knew." Daphne visited TPIC with a friend and enjoyed the service. She started regularly attending TPIC and MIC parenting classes. She got clean and sober through the ongoing support of MIC and the church and eventually regained custody of her daughter. "Through what I learned at MIC and TPIC, I began to live a drug-free life," she says. "Since then I have been clean for more than thirteen years. Thank God my dreams came true!"

Despite successes like these, several years after starting TPIC, my life and ministry took a tailspin that tested and tried my faith like never before. It was during that season of life I truly learned hope is like helium in my balloon of faith. Hope kept me afloat during the tough times I faced when both my personal and professional life were turned upside down.

PART II

11

The Hurricanes of Life

In 2005, the same year Hurricane Katrina devastated the Gulf Coast from Florida to Texas, a personal hurricane blew my way when I got married for all the wrong reasons.

I lost count of all the people who'd told me I needed a husband and how good it would be when I got married. It seemed that others felt something was wrong with me for being happily single and "married to the Lord," as I often claimed. I had a very strong, intimate relationship with the Lord and great friendships with the women who worked at MIC. After what had happened with Sam and Robert, I really wasn't looking for a husband. Instead, one found me.

I wasn't using drugs when Charles came along, but I was dealing with issues from my past that were causing me difficulty. Charles joined TPIC as a minister and told me he was interested in dating me. I decided that since everyone said I needed a husband, I'd give him a chance. We dated for a brief period before I acquiesced to his advances and accepted his marriage proposal, convincing myself our marriage was the will of God.

What I *didn't* know was that severe head trauma had left Charles incapacitated in many areas. I did know he had been in recovery from drug and alcohol abuse when he was involved in a terrible car accident that literally changed his life. He'd had to be cut out of the car, and while in the hospital, he'd given his life to Jesus. After that, Charles was a changed man. He went from selling and using drugs to carrying the gospel.

Charles and I married, and I endured much turmoil from his mood swings and erratic behavior. Finally, a year later, he showed me the medical records that identified his irreversible brain injury. Feeling undone, I asked Charles why he hadn't shown me the records before we'd married. He said he'd thought I wouldn't marry him if I had known the extent of his brain injury.

Even after finding out about Charles's condition, I tried to make the marriage work. I signed up for some brain-injury support groups and was really hoping for the best when Charles asked me for a divorce. He claimed he had to divorce me legally to keep his disability checks but that we could remain together in a common-law marriage—even though common-law marriage is not recognized in Florida. He said we didn't have to tell anyone; we could pretend we were still married.

At first I told Charles I would go along with this arrangement. I had borrowed money from him for MIC, and I felt obligated to him. After praying about it, though, I knew I couldn't do it. When I told Charles I didn't want a divorce, he turned very cold toward me and began making up lies about me. He told everyone who would listen that I was having an affair with a fellow minister and that this minister had "taken [his] wife and [his] church." I'll never forget one day after church services when Charles said to me in a menacing voice, "Game knows game."

Charles began slamming doors and looking quite intimidating as he walked around the house and TPIC. One day, as he left TPIC, he slammed the door so hard all the pictures and mirrors on the walls shook, and everyone was afraid he was going to come back and kill us all. Although Charles never physically abused me, but the emotional abuse took a toll, and my stomach would twist into knots whenever I heard his truck pull into the driveway. I began avoiding him by hiding in another room in the house.

I finally grew tired of the drama, retained an attorney, and authorized her to handle the divorce proceedings on my end. Charles divorced me in 2008. We were married for only three years, but it seemed more like thirty-three.

After the divorce, I felt that my hope for a good marriage was gone forever, but I kept my faith in God. I trusted he would "[make] everything beautiful in its time," as promised in Ecclesiastes 3:11 (NIV). He did, but not before I had faced more losses as the hurricanes of life continued to blow my way.

12

Everything That Can Be Shaken Is Shaken

The year 2008 was especially difficult for me: I lost not only my marriage but my mother. She had been an intricate and essential part of Janar's life and mine. After my stepfather died of complications from diabetes, Janar and I visited Mommy from time to time in Pensacola, where she was living alone. During one visit, she told me she had eased her profound loneliness by talking to a lizard. I knew my mother was a kindhearted animal lover, but this wasn't acceptable. On another visit, when she asked me whether she would be going to a nursing home, I knew I had to move her to Tallahassee with us.

Mommy sold her home, and I built a mother-in-law suite onto my home, where she lived and was well taken care of for her last seven years. She loved the Lord, and it was important to her to remain active in her African Methodist Episcopal Church, so she attended both her AME Church and TPIC every Sunday. My mother was so proud of how God had changed my life and how he was using me in MIC and TPIC. I told her she was my number-one fan. When I saw her smiling face in the congregation every Sunday, I felt such joy.

My mother loved children and worked with them all her life. Until she retired, she owned Wee Wise Owl, a preschool in Pensacola she bought when I was only ten. I remember going there every morning before school and coming there every day after school, as my mother worked sunup to sundown. When she came to live with Janar and me, she became a senior volunteer at a school for disabled children. She loved those beautiful children and talked about them every day. As a result, we knew the names of all her students and the various things they did.

My mother and Janar were very close. When I gave birth to Janar by cesarean section, my mother was in the operating room, and she held Janar before I did. She was heading out the door with Janar when I said, "Hey, wait, I want to see my baby." When Janar was a baby and I had to travel out of town, my mother and stepfather kept her for me, so when Janar got pregnant with my first granddaughter, Tayla, my mother was so excited.

I took my mother to the hospital a few days after Tayla was born so Mommy could meet her. Then I left to attend a meeting, only for Janar to call and tell me Mommy was sick. I couldn't believe it. I immediately returned to the hospital, and they admitted my mother because of her age. She had eaten some fish earlier that day, and I thought that maybe the fish had been bad. That night I prayed with her, sang hymns, and quoted scripture. I then said good night and went home. The next day was Sunday, and I had to preach at TPIC. I also had to finish preparing for Janar and Tayla to come home from the hospital the next day. I had no way of knowing that that was the last time I would see my mother alive. She died the next day of pulmonary aspiration.

I cried my eyes out; so did Janar. We remembered how my mother had told us on quite a few occasions that she was ready to go to heaven to see her identical twin, Elouise; her husband, Charles; her niece Laverne; her brother, Walter; her mother, Edna; and other family members. Even though we would miss her so much, we knew she was ready.

My mother was forty-one when I was born and eighty-five when she died. Losing her hurt me to the core, and I still think of her often. When

I think of my mother now, I smile through my tears as I remember how she was always there for me throughout my life, addiction, and recovery.

Not long after my mother passed, I started experiencing heavy bleeding and excruciating pain during my menstrual cycle. It got to the point where I bled for weeks at a time. I had to go to the emergency room several times because the bleeding wouldn't stop. I eventually went to my family doctor and friend, Dr. Cynthia Kimble, who recommended some laboratory tests. Those tests revealed that I had fibroid tumors that were growing and getting progressively worse. Dr. Kimble referred me to a gynecologist, who told me I needed surgery to remove the fibroids. I did not have health insurance at the time, so I wasn't able to have the surgery for a year.

That was a hard year of heavy bleeding and pain every month; it literally felt like labor pains. Despite wearing adult diapers and heavy-flow pads during my menstrual period, I still often bled through to my clothes. One Sunday, attendees had to literally carry me out of the sanctuary during one of my messages. I knew then that I had to have surgery without further delay.

At the hospital, I told an administrator about my condition and that I didn't have insurance. I showed her how often I had gone to the emergency room and what it had cost. I explained I would have to continue to do that unless I got the surgery. I even told her I had a physician who was willing to perform the surgery but that I needed a payment plan for the hospital costs. I thank God the hospital agreed to work with me so I could finally have the surgery.

Amid my personal crises, the nation was experiencing the financial crisis many economists considered the worst since the Great Depression. At that time, MIC was receiving grants from the city, county, and state and from United Way. We were also receiving contract funding to implement the Parents in Partnership Project, the Kids in Partnership Project, the Women Helping Women Jail Project, and other initiatives. When the economy collapsed, the money began to dry up, and we made an executive decision to stop applying for all grant funding. We believed strongly that MIC would continue with or without grants. Everything became volunteer oriented as we kept providing supportive services to the families who came to us. We lost the MIC house and moved our offices to TPIC, where they remain to this day.

Although I lost my job as executive director and grants manager for MIC, I did remain president of the nonprofit corporation. But that was not a paid position, and without paid employment, I did not know how I was going to take care of myself. At least I didn't have to worry about Janar and Tayla. Janar had moved away from home and graduated from college and was now working as a first-grade teacher in the Leon County School System. Brian, Tayla's father, was helping support both Janar and Tayla, and they were doing fine.

The first thing I did was enroll in the Institute for Life Coach Training at the recommendation of Dr. Mark Chironna, who was my bishop at the time. He is a master life coach, and he thought that I would be a good life coach. I took the forty-hour foundational course and fell in love with life coaching. I liked the synergy between coach and client, and I also liked the fact that a life coach helps people tap into their strengths and move forward in life. That represented hope to me, and I knew the power of hope, so I became a life coach and started coaching a few clients. I also wrote *You Are Beautiful: Unlocking Beauty from Within*. In addition, I signed up with a network-marketing coffee company with actor Danny Glover as one of my business partners. Although I didn't make much money selling coffee, I had a lot of fun traveling with Danny Glover and the rest of our team.

Still, I had what seemed like tons of bills hanging over me; they included my personal bills and the bills for MIC I had undersigned. I was trying to keep everything afloat, but it was an impossible task. Bill collectors were calling day and night. I decided to take a position working as a weight-loss consultant with Jenny Craig and file for bankruptcy. I had previously been a client with Jenny Craig and lost thirty pounds, so working for the organization was my way of giving back while learning how to keep the weight off. It also prepared me for an upcoming initiative of

MIC, Losing Weight and Loving Life, a support group that helps women lose excess weight and maintain healthy weight.

I could no longer afford to pay the mortgage on my home, so I had to turn it back over to the bank during the bankruptcy proceedings. It was hard for me to let it go as I thought about all the years I lived there while taking care of Janar and my mother. However, it was easier for me to let go of it after two break-ins.

My house was located on a relatively secluded street on the south side of town. Across the street from my house was a wooded lot where owls gathered at night. People also had to come into the neighborhood intentionally looking for my home because the street name was different on opposite ends of the street. Before cars and cell phones had GPS, even ambulance drivers and police had a hard time finding addresses there. During the last five of the fifteen years we lived on that street, the neighborhood declined and there were many abandoned homes, including one right next to mine. The family who had lived there throughout the years had a boy named Leon around Janar's age and a little girl named Chloe. They often played in the yard together while growing up.

The first burglary took place while I was on a trip to Atlanta. Millie Poulos of MIC was renting the suite my mother used to live in, and even though Millie was in town, someone came into my bedroom through a window that wasn't locked properly and stole my flat-screen television. I reported it to the police, to no avail. That break-in was inconsequential and free of drama, but I did feel violated.

The second break-in, however, *was* filled with drama, and I'll never forget it. Janar and her fiancé, Brian, were getting married the next day, and I was going to perform the ceremony. Millie and I had gone to the wedding rehearsal, and afterward, she went to run errands while I went home.

When I got home, the back door looked as though it wasn't closed all the way. It was locked, though, so I unlocked it and entered the house. When I walked into the kitchen, I stopped dead in my tracks: one of the large back windows in the kitchen had been broken out. As I walked through the house, I found that my laptop was missing, as was my Bible—it had been in a case that looked like a purse. I went back to the kitchen to examine the window and noticed blood. It seemed the burglar had cut himself while climbing through the broken glass.

I walked outside and called 911. I then called a friend and was telling him about what had happened when Leon, the little boy who used to live next door, appeared behind me. He was now a scary-looking grown man who was talking very fast as he approached. I immediately began describing him to my friend on the phone, and Leon stepped back. He said he'd been walking by when he'd heard me talking about a break-in. He said he might know who'd done it and could possibly help me get my laptop back—for a price, of course.

Leon left me his cell phone number, and a policeman eventually came. I told him I suspected Leon had been the one to break into my house, and I gave the policeman Leon's number. I also told him about the blood on the glass. Friends came over, we boarded up the back window, called Leon, and went on a wild goose chase trying to retrieve my laptop from him. I must have really wanted it back, because we met him at a shady trailer park and actually gave him thirty dollars. Leon took the money and never came back.

Many years later, I received a call from the state attorney's office: DNA evidence had proved Leon was indeed the person who had burglarized my house. The office was calling to let me know Leon was in jail for murdering someone at that same shady trailer park where my friends and I had met him. I believe God protected me on the day of the break-in because Leon didn't step away from me until he heard me describing him to my friend on the phone, and my friends and I were safe as we met Leon at the trailer park.

I experienced so much loss during that season that I felt as if I was being stripped of everything. Times were extremely rough and confusing, and I wondered what on earth was going on, but through it all, I remained clean and sober. This wasn't easy, because people close to me were turning to alcohol. For example, during that time, Nettie Walker Palmore of MIC started drinking and using drugs again after being clean for fifteen years.

I knew that that was not an option for me because I remembered the suffering and pain drugs and alcohol caused me. Therefore, I maintained my faith, hope, and love, and I believed everything was going to be all right.

Hope propelled me to continue and not to give up when everything inside me wanted to quit. I'd been through many hard times in my life before, and I knew that the trouble would not be permanent. My main objective was to hold on to hope until the situation got better.

13

The Nations Are Calling

With all the personal and professional challenges and changes taking place in my life, I started asking the Lord for my next assignment. I was in a time of transition, and just as with natural childbirth, it was both painful and exciting.

The answer to my prayers came in a unique way. In the middle of a message I was delivering at TPIC, I started talking about how I wanted to go to Africa. I didn't know anyone who lived there, nor did I know anyone who had traveled there, but I had a strong desire to go. Not long after that, I met Bishop Shirley Holloway from Washington, DC. I joined her ministry for a short period and learned that she went to Africa quite often. We shared a common interest in working with drug addicts; she had a major residential treatment program Nettie had entered when she relapsed.

I took my first trip to East Africa with Bishop Holloway. We traveled to Nairobi and to Kisumu, Kenya; the Republic of Burundi; and Kigali, Rwanda. When I arrived in Nairobi, my two large suitcases of clothes were missing. Our many trips to the airport were to no avail. In fact, I didn't receive my luggage until months after I returned to the United States—and I am told it's a miracle I got them back at all.

I fell in love with the people of Africa as I assisted Bishop Shirley while she ministered in various churches and crusades. One crusade I will never forget was held in the large Uhuru Park in Nairobi. The church was having its annual open-air deliverance service, and thousands of people were in attendance. As the local pastor prayed, many people started making noises with contorted faces, much like the little girl in the *Exorcist*. They were literally thrown onto the stage where we were standing, and we were asked to pray for them.

At first I was afraid, but then I noticed that as we prayed and showed these people the love of Christ, many were set free. A particular young lady really touched my heart. When she was first thrown onto the stage, Bishop Holloway attempted to pray for her, but the young lady started swinging her arms and acting aggressively. Bishop Holloway asked me to hug the young lady and pray for her. As I hugged her and prayed, she melted into my arms. That night, we prayed for thousands just like her, and I saw the power of God and love in action as we ministered hope to them. The metamorphosis from scowling and riotous behavior to quiet, calm, and peace was simply amazing.

That was my first visit to East Africa but not my last. Since then I have traveled back to East Africa, to South Africa, and to other countries I will tell about later.

14

The Tide Is Turning

After losing my home, I needed somewhere to stay, so I asked a woman from TPIC if I could rent a room from her. She lived in a nice three-bedroom home, and she allowed me to rent one of her rooms. I put the rest of my things into storage and lived with her for a little over a year.

As my life slowed down tremendously, I began to focus more on the things of God. I was still senior pastor at TPIC, and I conducted Sunday-morning worship services and Wednesday-night Bible study. In addition, I worked eight hours a day at Jenny Craig. When I wasn't working there, I stayed at the church all day long and well into the night. I then went to the gym and back to the small room I was renting. I also spoke at other churches and events from time to time.

Two significant things happened during this season. One was the acceptance of my calling as apostle. I ran from that call much as I had run from being a pastor. But this new calling had been prophesied on several occasions, and I was already functioning as an apostle—a "sent one" called to establish MIC and TPIC and, later, to work in Africa—but I didn't feel I needed the title. It wasn't until I went through this time of being stripped of everything and totally depending on the Lord that I truly received the spiritual office of apostle.

I finally realized that in the kingdom of God, promotion comes through suffering and humility as you endure trials and tests and come out refined, like pure gold. Through my suffering, I heard the Lord tell me I was his apostle, and I said yes to the call. One thing I learned a long time ago was that the Lord always gets his way!

The next significant occurrence was receiving an honorary doctorate in humanities from Bishop Gregory Wright, founding chancellor of the Five-Fold Ministry Theological University. I met Bishop Wright while speaking at a Preach the Word Worldwide Network TV event where I talked about the work I had done in MIC the past two decades. Bishop Wright called me several days after the event and asked to meet with me. When we met, he told me his theological university in Southern California gave out honorary doctorate degrees to those who had earned them through their ministry work over time. I sent him a packet with all the required documentation, and he came to Tallahassee to conduct the graduation ceremony.

Friends and colleagues from near and far came to attend the service. I remember crying tears of joy and amazement because I felt that God was honoring all the work I had done in establishing MIC and helping thousands of women and families for more than two decades. That's what I believe an honorary degree is all about: earned honor. When people call me *Dr. Rosalind* or *Apostle*, I don't feel puffed up or like a fraud; instead, I say to myself, "You see my glory, but you don't know my story." Incidentally, I also love being called by my birth name, Rosalind, which means "beautiful rose."

I eventually resigned from Jenny Craig to write my next book, *What Is It? Defining, Finding, and Obtaining Your It.* I also reconnected with my spiritual father, Dr. Steven Govender. He and his wife, Nancy, and their two children had come to the United States as missionaries from South Africa in the 1990s. When I first met Dr. Govender, I was surprised to hear he was from South Africa, because he did not look like Nelson Mandela. I found out later that his ancestors were from India.

A little background about my relationship with the Govenders is in order. We met while I was a member of Christian Victory Fellowship (CVF) Church. Dr. Govender conducted revival meetings on numerous occasions during the Refreshing and Renewal Revivals of the 1990s. There was always a mighty display of God's Spirit when he came, and I experienced God in unique ways during his services as I was filled with immense joy and hope.

On a deep spiritual level, God revealed to me that Dr. Govender was my spiritual father. As a matter of fact, when my friends and I decided to start TPIC, several women and I went to Louisiana to find Dr. Govender and ask him to be our spiritual covering. However, it was not the right time, and we did not reconnect until many years later.

Our reconnection happened early one morning while Millie and I were praying. Suddenly, Dr. Govender came to mind, and I asked Millie if she remembered him. She said, "Of course—how can one forget Dr. Govender?" Right then and there, we decided to look him up on Facebook. (Don't you just love the era of social media, where you can find just about anybody?) Fortunately, we found him, and we invited the Govenders to be our guests at TPIC's thirteenth-anniversary service. They came, and we were reunited in the unity of the Spirit in the bond of peace, and they became our spiritual covering.

The Govenders were then living in California. A couple years later, they decided to move back to South Africa after being away from their country of origin for two decades. Though none of us knew it at the time, this decision would have important consequences for me.

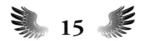

15

Throwing Back the Catfish

Around this time, I was mentoring a group of young-adult women from TPIC called Young Sisters in Success, and one of the young ladies asked me about online dating. Online dating was new to me, and I didn't want to advise her one way or the other because I really didn't have any experience with it. The things I had heard about online dating were not very positive, some of them downright scary. For instance, I was familiar with the television show *Catfish* and had watched several episodes. To be catfished is to be lured by someone into a relationship by means of a fictional online persona. The founder of the show had been catfished by an older woman pretending to be young and beautiful. The show demonstrated how being catfished was a heartbreaking experience some people never got over. It naturally made me suspicious of online dating.

In order to give the young women an informed answer about online dating based on more than a television show, I prayed about it and decided to sign up on a dating website. After all, I was single, had plenty of time on my hands, and considered it an adventurous research project.

I signed up for eharmony because I was familiar with the work of one of the founders, Neil Clark Warren, and I'd used his book *Love the Life*

You Live in my life-coach practice as recommended reading. I created my eharmony profile and shared that I was a pastor and that I didn't drink alcohol or use drugs. I included my photo, and I was honest and forthcoming with my answers. I liked the fact that eharmony used your profile to match your personality with others based on their assessment scales.

Despite all my precautions, the first guy I started talking with turned out to be a catfish! I spoke with him often on the telephone, and he had a Dutch accent, but he would never video chat with me. I asked him about Skype, and he claimed his computer's camera was broken. I should have known something was amiss, but we talked for long periods of time just about every day. Then one day, I got an email from eharmony: they said they had found out that this man wasn't who he said he was and that I should cut off all contact with him. The next time he called, I said, "I don't know who you really are, but you need to stop pretending. And please lose my telephone number."

The whole experience did turn out to be an adventure—more like the 1972 disaster film *The Poseidon Adventure*—and I thought it was over. I stopped going to the eharmony website, but I decided to leave my profile up until my contract ended. After all, I reasoned, it was already paid for. I just prayed about it and left it alone. I had peace about the whole experience, I didn't feel devasted, and simply chalked it up to research.

16

Making a Love Connection

Even when Dr. Govender decided to move his family back to South Africa, we stayed in touch. In the summer of 2013, he asked me to come to Durban during South Africa's Women's Month (August) to speak at various churches and events. I was excited about traveling to Africa once again and eagerly accepted. The woman from whom I was renting a room went to South Africa with me, and I told my story of hope at several churches. I met many wonderful people while in South Africa, including a young man named Jonathan Annipen. Because of our friendship, I traveled back to Durban on several occasions.

The night before returning to America, I had a very interesting and impactful dream. In the dream, I was walking down the aisle of a huge throne room in heaven, wearing a shimmering, evanescent, yellow-and-gold-and-beige wedding gown. It had long, flowing sleeves with crystal rhinestones that reflected bright light that emanated from Jesus, who was standing at the end of the aisle waiting for me. Beautiful worship music was playing, and when I got to where he was standing, we started dancing all around heaven.

When I woke up, the dream felt so real it seemed it had really happened. At the time, I interpreted the dream to mean I had had a ceremony in heaven and married the Lord. When I returned to America, I told all my friends and ministry-team members about the dream and that I believed I was officially married to the Lord. I asked them to stop praying for a husband for me, and they agreed to.

Approximately two weeks after returning from South Africa, I received an email from a man on eharmony. By that time, I had forgotten my profile was still up. I was about to delete the email, but something about the photo in it made me stop and take a closer look. The man in the picture looked distinguished, like a college professor. I read the email, and I liked the questions he'd asked me. He seemed genuinely interested in getting to know the real me. That was refreshing because one of the things that had always concerned me about online dating was the fact that people seemed to be superficially sampling the goods, much like a bumblebee going from flower to flower.

The man told me that his name was Kwame, that he lived in Maryland, and that he worked for the federal government in information technology. We had very engaging email conversations: he was trying to get to know the essence of who I was, and I liked that he got to the heart of the matter. During this period, I sent him photos and videos from my recent trip to South Africa, and he stated he would love to travel to other countries one day as well.

Eventually we took the next step and started to communicate via telephone. When I first heard Kwame's voice, I was surprised by his accent. I had assumed he was from the United States, but that was clearly not the case. He was from Guyana, a country in South America; he had grown up there but had come to the United States to attend school and decided to make this country his home. The more we spoke on the telephone, the more Kwame's voice became a sweet melody to me. If it was edible, it would be dark-chocolate-covered raisins, sweet and rich, the kind that make you want to eat a whole one-pound bag in one sitting.

Kwame became more and more endeared to me, and I asked if he wanted to start using Skype to video chat. When he said he wasn't on Skype, I became suspicious because of the catfish I had encountered on eharmony. But the next time we spoke, Kwame had signed up for Skype, and he asked if I wanted to video chat. Surprised, I said yes—until I looked in the mirror and realized I didn't look my best, so I told him we should plan to Skype another time. After that, we started video chatting on a regular basis, and things went smoothly.

As I approached my fiftieth birthday, I asked Kwame to come and share it with me. I told him we could travel to Destin Beach, Florida, one of my all-time favorite places, and spend time getting to know each other. We both agreed that we would keep it G-rated.

The first time I saw Kwame in person (we'd now been corresponding with one another for two months), it was like moving from analog television to high-definition digital. I liked that he dressed like a gentleman, and I was able to see his grayish-brown eyes up close and personal. Although he was shorter than he appeared in his photos, he was taller than me and very fit. He told me he had run track for many years while in school and now worked out at the gym. I must say I liked what I saw, and I was pleased to know he liked what he saw in me as well. He said he particularly liked my eyes and smile.

I remembered the dream I had had in South Africa of me in a wedding gown in heaven, and I realized that the interpretation was different than I had first believed. However, I was a little anxious about introducing Kwame to my daughter and friends, because they were the ones whom I had told to stop praying for a husband for me. Nevertheless, we all went out to dinner for my birthday, where I introduced Kwame to everyone. After dinner, Janar and my friends gave me the thumbs-up and said that there seemed to be chemistry between Kwame and me. I was especially relieved that Janar liked him.

The next time Kwame and I met in person was at Thanksgiving, when I traveled to Maryland. I was still renting the room in Tallahassee, so when I entered Kwame's five-thousand-square-foot house, I felt as though I was in the Taj Mahal! He kept it very nice and was really pleased with it. He left me there while he went to work for the two days before Thanksgiving. I was happy because it gave me a chance to investigate every inch of the house, from the basement to the second floor, as I walked around and prayed.

While I was walking and praying, I discerned that Kwame was hiding something from me. When he came home from work on the second day, I asked him to please come and sit down. He did, and I told him I was upset and wanted to go back to Tallahassee. He calmly asked what was wrong. I looked him in the eye and asked him to please be honest with me. Kwame said he would. I explained that as I was walking and praying around his home, I received the distinct impression that he had a ministry call. He just looked at me for a while, then said he did believe he had been called as a young boy but had veered away from that path in pursuit of worldly success.

The reason I was so upset was that after my failed marriage, I had vowed I would not get involved with another minister. There had always been conflict and competition between Charles and me when it came to ministry. He believed that because he was a man, he should be over the ministry to which God had called me, and I did not believe that to be true. In fact, I had encountered many churches with male ministers who thought women should not pastor at church or in leadership in the ministry. I had even believed that same thing until God had called me into the ministry.

When I first met Kwame, I was happy he wasn't in the ministry, and I thought that he was just a wonderful man who also shared my faith. I didn't know he had also had a call. Now he held me as I cried, and he assured me that whatever we did, we would do it together. I decided to stay, and I'm glad I did.

KWAME'S STORY

Kwame's full name is Richard Lester Kwame Lewis, and he was born in Guyana, South America. He had been studious early in life, and at a young age, he wrote prayers and placed them on the walls of his bedroom. He also diligently read the Bible, always seeking knowledge.

Kwame earned academic scholarships in high school and was accepted to the University of Illinois to study actuarial science. According to his own assessment, all of that was short-circuited during his teen years, when he started seeking knowledge away from God and living a worldly life. He pursued success through education, work, and money. He got married, worked good jobs, started a family, and bought houses and cars. Through all this, he was missing and thinking of the boy who wrote prayers, and he lost hope.

Two wonderful children, houses, and cars could not keep him married, and he was divorced twice. During his first divorce proceeding, he missed a court hearing, and a bench warrant was issued. He was arrested and spent several hours in jail waiting on the night judge. He acknowledges that this humbled him and reminded him of his early years in the United States, when he slept on the floor while going to college. Kwame had thought he was beyond such humiliation, but he shared, "A good friend, who was a believer in Christ, told me that God had to sit my ass down because he wanted my attention. He got it, and I am glad he did!"

After his second marriage collapsed, Kwame finally took the time to be still, and his journey back to hope began. He started studying the works of Dr. Wayne Dyer, Zen meditation, Buddhism, Islam, Hinduism, shamanism, yoga, chakras, and finally the mega churches with thousands of members. But he still felt empty after all that study, and he experienced no life-empowering hopefulness.

Finally, one day in February 2011, while Kwame was having his morning coffee in his beautiful home, he states, "I felt the touch of the Lord, and I looked up and said, 'It was always you.' His touch was gentle, soft but so powerful, until I fell to the floor sobbing. I prayed and asked Jesus to be the Lord of my life, and I began a biblical journey. After this experience, I was filled with life and hope every time I read the Bible."

Two years later, Kwame and I met, and that journey continued.

17

Marriage and Ministry

On Thanksgiving morning, a few days after the discussion and resolution about his calling into the ministry, Kwame presented me with an engagement ring and asked me to marry him. I had known him only three months, but I knew he was the one, so I said yes. At last, my love had come along.

We had a short engagement and got married three months later, after I introduced him to Dr. Govender. It was important to me that my spiritual father approve of Kwame. He did. Dr. Govender and Pastor Nancy came to Tallahassee and performed the ceremony.

I had known Kwame a whopping six months, but it seemed as though I had known him most of my life because we became fast friends who genuinely liked being with each other. The only problem was that he still lived in Maryland and I lived in Tallahassee. We discussed and prayed about where we would live together. I had moved out of the single room I was renting and into a nice two-bedroom apartment, but I was very content living either there or in Maryland. For the time being, Kwame traveled back and forth, driving thirteen hours to Tallahassee, staying for a few days, and then returning to Maryland.

After several months of that, Kwame started a new IT business I named Divine Design Mastermind IT Project Management (DDMITPM). He sent out notices to companies in Tallahassee about the project-management services he was offering. About three months later, he had an interview to partner with a company that contracted with that state government. We prayed and asked the Lord if it was his will to open that door. The door opened, and Kwame partnered with the company and started working on a major project with the Department of Education in Tallahassee. The guiding light for us was TPIC because Kwame loved being a part of the chapel outreach of MIC. He said he liked the fact that he could finally pursue his desire to serve in the ministry.

Kwame and I had been married for only six months when we took our first overseas trip together. I was invited by Jonathan Annipen, whom I had met on my first trip to Durban, to come to South Africa again in August for Women's Month. He scheduled an extensive ministry speaking tour that included traveling to several locations from Durban to Richards Bay, back to Durban, and then to Cape Town. I believe traveling to another country on such an ambitious ministry tour enhanced our marriage in many ways. It added substance that often comes only with time.

While ministering overseas, Kwame learned that the first lesson of ministry is servanthood. He served me in the ministry, and he also served me personally because I got sick. I picked up a nasty bug that caused me to lose my voice, and by the time we made it to Cape Town, all I could do was sleep during the day and then go and speak at the services at night. I woke up in pools of sweat from perspiring profusely throughout the night. Kwame cared for me and was by my side through it all. I fell deeper in love with him as I received his genuine love and affection.

Kwame nursed me back to health, and that was no small task. I remember one time when I was in the bathroom trying to pull myself together. My body was aching so badly I looked up to heaven and said I was ready to die if it was my time. I'm so glad it wasn't! After that first trip, despite the difficulties, we inherently knew that God was calling us as a ministry team.

The next overseas trip came approximately five months later, when we took a mission trip to Istanbul, Turkey, with Dr. Patricia Bailey's Master's Touch Ministries (MTM). Our team joined with a local pastor and provided supplies to Syrian refugees who were living in tents on the border. I was especially affected by the babies who were living in the tents with their families.

One day, we were passing out food, clothes, flashlights, heaters, and other supplies. The sun was going down, so we had to hurry. At one point, the women came out of the tents holding their beautiful babies, all of whom were crying. They brought their babies to me and were speaking in Arabic. I didn't know what they were saying until an interpreter explained that the babies were teething and the mothers wanted to know if we had something for their gums. Unfortunately, we did not, but I held the babies and prayed for them.

We also ministered in churches and homes with refugees who had fled religious persecution in Iran and Iraq. On one occasion, we met a young woman who had fled Iraq for religious asylum after she had accepted Jesus. She had had to leave her son with his father. Her mother was also a Christian, and her father wasn't quite convinced, but he was with her in Turkey. She was very broken but completely committed to her new faith in Christ, and she was looking for ways to be reunited with her son. I will never forget when we went to a service in her home one night. The tiny apartment was filled with her friends and neighbors. They cooked bread and other ethnic dishes and fed us well. I knew I was in the right place when we entered her sparsely furnished apartment and saw these three words written on the only poster on the walls: *There Is Hope*.

In December 2015, Kwame and I went on another mission trip with MTM to the Democratic Republic of the Congo to bring Christmas to the people there. While on this mission trip, we visited a rape crisis center located deep in the jungle, close to the border, where tribal warfare was taking place. It was a stark, gray, concrete building surrounded by a barbed-wire fence. The center housed women and children who were victims of rape. Many people don't know that rape is often used as a weapon during war. After the women at this center had been raped, their families no longer wanted them, and they were cast out of their villages. The women ranged in age from teenagers to senior citizens, and many had their children with them. They were beautiful, passionate women who sang and danced their greetings to us.

One night, the women from our mission team spent the night in the shelter and slept where the women slept. It was a difficult night for me because as I lay in that little bed on the cement floor, it was as though I felt all the pain and rejection that the center's women had experienced. I cried all night.

The next morning, we arose early and went to a morning worship service with the women. They praised the Lord with a purity and power I'd never seen. We gave them gift bags filled with cell phones, hygiene products, and other items. We also brought dolls, yellow rubber ducks, and other gifts for the children. I will never forget that when we gave the gift bags to the women, they praised God in their native tongue for a full fifteen minutes before they even opened the gifts. When we asked what they were saying, the interpreter told us they were thanking us for the gifts and praying for God to bless us. I learned a true lesson in gratitude while watching those women.

Another highlight of the DRC experience came when Kwame and one of the other men traveling with us were asked to address the women. Kwame stood in front of the women and asked them to forgive him on behalf of the men who had raped them. He shared his apology with sincerity and love. The women were visibly moved as they looked on him with pain and anger. In that moment, Kwame became a scapegoat, and he broke down and cried. As I hugged him and prayed, the women began to cry, and they received another level of healing that day. They told us that no man had ever apologized to them for the atrocious experiences that had happened to them. It was very moving and powerful to experience the love of God in action.

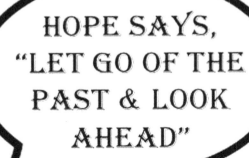

18

Immersed in Hope

When MIC celebrated its twenty-fifth anniversary, I was delighted and excited about the next chapter in our journey. I thought about the young woman I had been when I'd received the vision in 1991 and how I'd been so green I hadn't even known what a ministry was. Here we were, twenty-five years later, receiving proclamations from both the city of Tallahassee and Leon County commissioners to honor us for helping more than ten thousand families over the years.

As we were preparing for the celebration, God gave MIC's Christ Vision Tribe (CVT)—the envisioning arm that meets every week to strategize and organize ways to spread hope; the Hope Squad is the team that goes out and implements the plans—our next assignment: we asked for and received proclamations from both the city and county commissions designating every Friday as HOPE Universe Day, a day to share hope and smiles with those in need. It was mainly a goodwill gesture, but we were earnest about spreading hope on Fridays among families and communities, one person at a time. HOPE stands for Helping Others Practice Empowerment. MIC organized the Hope Universe Grace Initiative (HUGI) to carry out the monumental task of spreading hope each Friday.

We kicked off the first Hope Universe Day outreach on April 22, 2016, at a Bishop T. D. Jakes conference in Orlando. During the conference that Friday, we sought out people with whom we could share hope and smiles. We told them who we were and what we were doing, videotaped the encounters, and gave each one a copy of my previous book in the hope series. It was a resounding success, and people were responsive to our message of hope; each one smiled and thanked us. One woman said, "You have made my day. I just received bad news from home, but you guys helped me to have hope. Thanks!"

After that success, we knew we were off to a great start, so we continued to organize events and to share hope on Fridays throughout the entire year. Each Hope Universe Day, we delivered messages of hope in person and on social media. In addition, MIC encouraged everyone to spread messages of hope on Fridays—such as "Hope, not hate," "Hope knows no color," "Hope for the future," and "Hope, not hype." We also encouraged others to share hope not only through words but through actions at home, in the marketplace, and in the community.

MIC celebrated Hope Universe Day by going to nursing homes, homeless shelters, elementary schools, community events, community parks, and other places every Friday to share hope and smiles. During the events we hosted, and in most of the places we went to, we shared our personal stories of hope and encouraged others to share theirs. Depending on the venue, we gave away clothes, food, and books, and lots of love.

Over the years, we even shared hope in other countries as we were privileged to go on a mission trip to Haiti with MTM. This was my first trip to Haiti, and Aaronetta Frison, one of the Citizens of Hope, accompanied me. On the Friday we were in Haiti, Aaronetta and I celebrated Hope Universe Day and gave out books. I also had the opportunity to share hope with a group of forty young women who had been displaced by the devastating earthquake that hit Haiti in 2010. The country was still recovering from the earthquake, and many of these women had suffered traumatic rape and other horrendous tribulations in the aftermath. In partnership with other organizations in a multiyear project, MTM worked with these women to empower them physically, emotionally, mentally, and spiritually.

I shared with the women inspirational thoughts from my book *You Are Beautiful: Unlocking Beauty from Within*. I told them they were beautiful just the way God had made them, and I gave them beauty affirmations to speak over themselves. I also shared poetry and had one-on-one sessions with a few of the women. One woman who really touched my heart was in an abusive relationship. She had a beautiful baby and was really in need of empowerment. I listened to her story via an interpreter and was able to lead her to Christ. I heard years later that through the support of the MTM project, this woman was doing great, had her own business, and had escaped that abusive relationship.

An especially emotional and impactful Hope Universe Day happened when the Hope Squad went to Orlando after the massacre at the Pulse nightclub in June 2016. Four of the Hope Squad members traveled five hours from Tallahassee to Orlando to share hope with a woman who'd lost her son in the attack. We arrived at the scene five days after the shooting, and the media, police, and many others still surrounded the nightclub. As we drove up to park in a lot a few blocks away, I felt sick; I felt an ache in my stomach and could hear in my mind the screams of the forty-nine people who had died. We parked, got out of our van, and walked up and down the block while praying. After that, we drove to a memorial site displaying photos of the victims who'd been killed; people were placing cards, flowers, and other items around the photos. We placed a Hope Certificate and flowers in front of the photo of the young man whose mother we knew.

We were wearing our Hope Squad T-shirts, and we noticed that people were curiously checking us out. We were quiet and respectful, and at one point we sat in the folding chairs, silently crying, as we faced the photos of the slain. We ended up sitting there for a while. As we were leaving, a couple who had traveled from New York City stopped us and asked who we were. As we shared our message of hope with them, they hugged us and told us they had lost their son in the shooting. They went on to tell us that our presence had made a big difference. I can truly say I saw the force of hope upheld by faith and love, the greatest being love.

In December 2016, Kwame and I traveled to Nairobi, Kenya, with MTM to spread hope to South Sudanese refugees facing a major crisis. South Sudan was in the middle of brutal tribal warfare that had forced thousands to flee their homes; many had ended up in refugee camps in Nairobi. We met with the churches who had organized and cared for the widows and orphans, and we brought them much-needed quantities of food, clothing, and other items. We also visited the local United Nations office and brought hope and help to orphanages and other places of need while there.

When I first saw the South Sudanese people, I was struck by how tall and regal they were. Their dignity shone even amid their challenging circumstances. The women were dressed in vibrant colors, and their dark skin was as beautiful and smooth as butter. The young men were tall and walked with strength and power. The South Sudanese are a welcoming and passionate people, and it was a humbling experience to be able to love them and receive love in return.

After celebrating Hope Universe Day every Friday for a little more than a year, MIC applied to the National Day Calendar and asked for the month of April to be designated as the National Month of Hope in the United States. I was surprised to learn that there wasn't already a national month of hope. We chose the month of April because the flowers are blooming once again and the butterflies are spreading their wings and flying high. April is the month of new beginnings and possibilities, and hope is in the air! It also happened to be the month I'd first conceived the idea for MIC.

Out of approximately eighteen thousand applications for that cycle, the National Day Calendar chose thirty, and MIC was one. The organization later told me that our application was chosen because of the organization's history of spreading hope. The National Day Calendar could see powerful stories of hope behind who we were and could tell our application wasn't just a gimmick to sell products.

We were excited about our month being chosen, and we began to plan for the first-ever National Month of Hope in April 2018. The challenge was to get the word out and make people aware that we now had a whole month in which to celebrate hope as a nation. At first, we came up with a list of activities in honor of the National Month of Hope. Most were the kinds of things we had done to celebrate Hope Universe Day. However, after much consideration, we realized that what we wanted people to do was a little more than just community outreach. Hope was about people's mindsets and how they saw the world, not about what they did. Therefore, we came up with a hope campaign encouraging people to make hope connections by thinking hope and having hope chats (which I explain later in this book).

To kick off the inaugural National Month of Hope, I started my Think Hope podcast and participated in a radio-show "hope tour," in which I was interviewed on various radio stations and podcasts in Los Angeles, New York, Iowa, Louisiana, and everywhere in between. It was an eye-opening experience to many people as I shared how America is facing a hope crisis: people are in despair to the point of taking their own lives. But I truly believe we can turn this trend around through the power of hope.

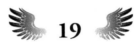

19

South African Hope Tour

During the early months of celebrating Hope Universe Day, in August 2016, I returned to Durban with a team that consisted of Kwame, Citizens of Hope, Dr. Brenda Jarmon, Aaronetta Frison, and Sharon Durham. I was once again asked to speak during South Africa's Women's Month at various churches, schools, shelters, and community events. It was a powerful time, as my entire team was committed to seeing the power of hope in action. I now refer to this trip as our South African Hope Tour.

The people of South Africa were gracious and welcomed our message of hope, as their country was facing major political and financial crises. I used the example of hope being like the helium in a balloon, and I shared the truth that hope has the power to cause your faith to rise and to take you high above all the trials and tribulations of life. Overall, the trip was a resounding success, and the message of hope we delivered in the universal language of love was well received. Not only did we share hope, we also received hope. We met someone at one of the churches who had a ship named *Hope* that traveled the world with teams of missionaries to provide help to those in need.

As I reflected on the South African Hope Tour, it struck me that God really does use each of us according to his plans and dictates. I would never have thought in a million years that God would send me to South Africa to meet with and minister to so many wonderful South Africans of Indian decent whose ancestors had arrived in the present-day province of KwaZulu-Natal 150 years ago from India. These immigrants served primarily as indentured laborers working hard on sugar farms. They were among the many groups discriminated against and mistreated during this time.

On our visit, we were blessed to be invited into many of the homes and churches of South Africans of Indian decent, and we were well fed. We particularly enjoyed the rich, spicy curry and tandoori and the delectable desserts. We were also delighted to learn about the rich heritage of this group of South Africans. We met and spoke with some of their prestigious political leaders, one of whom—the Honorable Sanklavathy Railbally, former member of the National Assembly of South Africa—fought alongside the late President Nelson Mandela in the struggle for equality.

God moved in mysterious ways as we prayed for and blessed the women, men, and children of South Africa. One powerful moment of hope came on the third night of our two-week tour. The host church was renting a tent for our visit, and everyone had to be out by a certain hour, but the church's three attendants picked up our team late. To make up for their tardiness, the attendants all drove extremely fast. We were riding in very nice cars—two BMWs and a Mercedes-Benz—but we could not enjoy the ride because of the speed! Kwame, the driver, and I prayed the whole time as we zipped off to the event.

By the time we got to the huge white tent, which was carpeted, insulated, and had heat and air conditioning, the hosts immediately ushered me up to the podium to preach. I literally felt as though I was flying. The atmosphere was charged with the power of the Holy Spirit, and I could tell that much prayer had taken place prior to our arrival. From the moment I opened my mouth to speak to the end of the powerful altar call, I was caught up in the glory of the Lord. It was a service I will never forget because of its intensity.

During that service, I shared the Bible story found in John 4, the account about the Samaritan woman who had an encounter with Jesus at the well. Jesus told her about the living water he had to give that would be like a well of water springing up eternally. I likened the springing up of this living water to hope. As you drink this living water, your hope in Christ Jesus will spring up and cause your faith to rise. That is what I believe happened to the Samaritan woman. As she spoke with Jesus and he prophetically told her about her life, she was drinking from the well of living water. This caused her hope to spring up to the point where her faith propelled her to run and tell everyone in her village to come and see Jesus.

Not only did I preach about the power of hope that night, but we also saw the power of hope in action, as many people came to the altar, where God touched them mightily. This happened again and again in churches all across Durban.

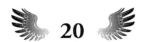

20

The Eight Pearls of Wisdom Revisited

In my previous book in this ongoing series on hope, I wrote:

> I am embarrassed to admit that it took all of the pain and suffering that I went through in order for me to finally surrender my will and my way unto God. However, I believe that my journey to the hellhole of addiction and all that came with it helped me to come out with what I call pearls of wisdom. The reason that I call them pearls of wisdom is because pearls are formed deep in the heart of the ocean, within the shells of oysters and other mollusks as they enclose irritating foreign objects. I found my greatest treasures in the midst of challenging and irritating circumstances. It was as though I was that foreign object enclosed in the hard shell of addiction.

The eight pearls of wisdom are powerful concepts that continue to affect my life and make me who I am today. They include the power of hope, the power of love, the power of prayer, the power of resilience, the power of unity, the power of humility, the power of passion, and the power of you. In this chapter, I revisit each of the pearls of wisdom from the per-spective of hope.

THE POWER OF HOPE

Hope is needed to sustain sanity in the face of suffering and pain, because hope is not just an emotion—it is an eternal force the Bible says shall remain forever (see 1 Corinthians 13:13). People often give up because they lose hope. Hopelessness is at the heart of all pessimistic thinking. Pessimism often leads to sarcasm. Pain is at the heart of sarcasm, and as that pain festers, it causes one to lash out at others.

Hope is for the future. Faith is for right now. That is why I have faith for now and hope for later. You can't have faith without hope; as the Bible says, "Now faith is the substance of things hoped for, the evidence of things not seen" (Hebrews 11:1, KJV). Faith is made of the substance of hope. This is what makes hope so powerful: no matter what is happen-ing right now, there is hope for tomorrow. Amid the darkness, hope is the light that guides the way. Just have faith and keep following the light of hope, and eventually you will reach your destination.

During the early years of MIC, I wrote several public-service announce-ments with a message of hope that aired on local television stations for more than a decade. Most of them ended with me saying, "Remember, as long as there is breath in your body, there is hope!" That is not just cliché. There *is* power in hope. Hopeless people do not have a reason to get up in the morning. They think, *What's the use?* Living becomes mundane and meaningless if there is not a brighter day on the horizon.

I have felt the sting and reality of hopelessness, despair, and mental illness on multiple occasions, for example, when one of the mothers who attended MIC committed suicide. She had come to MIC after seeing one of our public-service announcements. While attending our support groups, she had mentioned how the message of hope had motivated her on several occasions while she was up late at night getting high on crack cocaine. After completing her psychosocial assessment, we referred her to another program for mental-health counseling and recommended she go into a residential dual-diagnosis treatment program for women. She went but left the program prematurely; less than a week later, her body was found. She had taken a lethal dose of sleeping pills.

Many years later, I was directly confronted by a young woman I'll call Caroline, who was about to commit suicide. Caroline lives on an island in the Caribbean, and I met her online when she contacted me about a radio program I had done on the power of forgiveness. Caroline told me there were some things she could not forgive, and she proceeded to share with me that she had been sexually abused as a child. I listened intently to her and then told her I had gone through similar abuse. I prayed with her, and she decided to forgive.

We became Facebook friends, and I learned that Caroline is a very intelligent and beautiful young woman who can sing like a bird. However, she cut herself all over her body to relieve her emotional pain. I also learned she was in an extremely abusive relationship with a man who had raped her on several occasions, and she could not seem to get rid of him.

One day, I was at work when I got a message from Caroline's mother saying Caroline had locked herself in the bathroom and was about to end her life. I immediately contacted Caroline through Facebook Messenger and asked how she was doing. I was relieved when she responded. She said she was tired of living and just wanted to give up.

This young woman felt that suicide was her only way out. If she had been living in the United States, I could have called the authorities, who would have sent someone to Caroline's home. Because she was living in another country, I didn't have that option, so I continued to message her. I was relieved every time she responded. In my messages, I reminded Caroline about her plans to come to the United States and some of the things we were going to do. I also told her I loved her and that God loved her even more.

Suddenly, Caroline's mother messaged me: "What did you just say to her?"

I told her what I had said, and Caroline's mother told me her daughter had come out of the bathroom and looked a lot better. I cried tears of joy!

I continued to coach Caroline. Eventually she decided that life *is* worth living, and despite many ups and downs, she is doing well.

People who are suffering often ask, "Where is hope? I am going through hell, and I don't see, have, or feel hope!" I would like to answer that question with my poem "Where Is Hope?"

Hope is found in the breath that I breathe,
In the stars in the sky and in the cool of the breeze.
Hope is found in a baby's cry or tears rolling down the eye
Of one who knows that every good thing flows from the heart of God.
Hope is found in the birds that sing, in the grass as it grows,
In the smell of a rose, in the dew as it settles upon the ground.
Hope can be found in the middle of pain, in the streets of frustration,
And in the home of the Name that is above every Name!
Hope is found when you hear the Name, think the Name, or say
*   the Name.*
It's all the same
Because Jesus is hope!

I wrote that poem after listening to a discussion on National Public Radio. The guests were outlining current events and sharing their insights on issues relating to race and violence. As I sat listening, I asked myself what I would say if I were part of the discussion. As I got out of my car, I looked up and began to speak this poem in response. No matter how bad it looks, there is still hope, and we can find it not in anger, blaming, or rhetoric, but in life, love, and Jesus.

The meaning of the first part of the poem is that hope is all around us. Hope can be found in the common, simple things of life that we often overlook or take for granted. For example, when you take one breath, there is the implied hope that you will take another. When you look up in the night sky, the stars you see imply that light shines even in darkness.

A baby's cries indicate life. When you hear birds, see grass, smell roses, and feel dew, nature gives you a reason to sing. The second part of the poem implies that even in times of pain and frustration, hope can still be found in Jesus Christ.

We are the light of the world (see Matthew 5:14). I believe one of the ways in which we shine is by being the light of hope that guides people through hard times. We all have times in our lives filled with pain and despair. The important thing is to allow our pain to give birth to hope and not to hopelessness, shame, bitterness, and anger. These are a few of the many negative consequences that can come out of tough times. But the light of hope empowers us.

I am grateful that by the grace of God, I gave birth to hope through MIC. I was able to take all the negative energy stored up in my life and make something positive out of it.

The Bible says, "Which hope we have as an anchor of the soul, both sure and steadfast, and which entereth into that within the veil" (Hebrews 6:19, KJV). That is truly good news because there are times in all of our lives when our souls need to be anchored—and there could be no better anchor than Jesus and the power of hope.

THE POWER OF LOVE

The topic of love has been contemplated and written about since the beginning of time. Families have been formed and divided in the name of love. Wars have even been fought in the name of love. Yet people continue to ask what love is or why it's relevant.

According to the Bible, "God is love" (1 John 4:16, ESV)—and "love is patient . . . [and] kind, . . . keeps no record of wrongs, . . . [and] always perseveres" (1 Corinthians 13:4–7, NIV). In contrast to the biblical view, society's definitions of love are often based on the common myths about love we see in Hollywood movies or romance novels. They portray love in a cookie-cutter fashion in which boy meets girl, they "fall in love," they experience conflict, and ultimately, they get together and live happily ever after. While we may know that's largely a fantasy, somewhere deep inside we look for that kind of love—and we often misjudge the love we do have because it doesn't look like that "ideal love."

But there is no greater force than unconditional love. Unconditional love is the love that compelled God to send his Only Begotten Son into this world. Unconditional love is the love that compelled Jesus to die on the cross for our sins. That kind of love doesn't depend on what is inside the person *receiving* the love—instead, it depends on what is inside the person *giving* the love.

In my own journey, I had to learn how to love others "without hooks"—in other words, if I wanted to be loved unconditionally, I couldn't love others based on what they did or did not do. I had to learn how to forgive and release others and choose to love based on who I was and Whose I was. Because of this, I've seen the power of love in action time and time again. I have literally loved the hell out of many of the women with whom I've had the privilege of working over the years, and they were subsequently transformed by love. For them, just knowing I cared and pointed them to God made all the difference in the world.

I am a woman who loves deeply, and I enjoy making connections with others based on mutual love and respect. This kind of love came to me through my relationship with Christ, and it has carried me through many trials and tests. The Bible tells us that faith, hope, and love shall remain, "but the greatest of these is love" (1 Corinthians 13:13, NIV).

I have found that love is the anchor of my hope; I cannot have hope without love. This was highlighted in my life whenever I went through an economic downturn and didn't know what I was going to do with my life. I kept my loving relationship with the Lord strong, which helped me have faith and hope. I rejected the temptation to blame God and drop my faith, because I realized that the love of God was what would deliver me and bring me to a place of wholeness.

Love is the powerful force that has navigated me through myriad tough times. I was compelled to stop using drugs and alcohol because of the love I had and have for my daughters, Janadra and Janar. Janadra died because of my drug addiction, but as I carried Janar in my womb, I loved her and wanted to protect her from my addiction. Once she was born, it was love that constrained me to abstain from drugs. It was love that compelled me to help other women once I was clean. It is love that compels me to continue to share my story after all these years.

During my addiction, I was a selfish person. I thought only about what was in it for me. I didn't care how my actions affected those who loved me. It wasn't until Janar came along and I had to think about someone else's welfare that I began to be others-centered and not self-centered. I learned I could not truly love if it was all about me.

Love is unselfish, and *love* is action. If you truly love, you will lay down your life for your fellow man or woman. I appreciated the power of love once I learned how to love. It wasn't until then that I began to realize how my mother's love had helped me in so many ways. She loved me unconditionally and never gave up on me. That is one of the reasons MIC is so powerful: we provide unconditional love.

Forgiveness is an important part of love. Sometimes it is hard to forgive. I had to determine to forgive others of past injustices. Many of the women who are addicted to various substances have been the victims of sexual abuse. The guilt, shame, and blame one experiences in being sexually abused is enough to lead one into addiction. Even when one is sexually abused as a child, forgiveness needs to take place—not so much for the sake of the abuser as for the sake of the abused. As the saying goes, harboring unforgiveness is like drinking poison and waiting for the other person to die.

I was sexually abused as a child by my uncle, and I had to forgive. I even ended up leading that uncle to Christ while he was on his deathbed. He was dying of lung cancer when my aunt asked me to come and pray for him in the hospital; I believe she did so because I was a newly ordained minister and my family was very proud of me. When my aunt first made the request, thoughts of how my uncle had abused me rushed into my mind. I had to pray and ask God to help me. He did, and I drove to Pensacola from Tallahassee to see my uncle. When I walked into the hospital room and saw a mere shadow of the man my uncle had once been, my heart was moved with compassion, and I cried. I led him in the Sinner's Prayer and prayed for his soul to be saved. Two weeks later, he died.

When we refuse to forgive, our ability to love God and others is hindered. Forgiveness is a liberating experience. When we learn to forgive, we learn to love unconditionally and unselfishly. No one should allow abuse of any kind to continue, but forgiveness does need to take place.

As I continually learn how to love unconditionally despite all I have been through, my definition of love continues to evolve. And I have found that the best way to really experience love is moment by moment. I believe there are opportunities to love all around us every day. When we understand this, we realize we are blessed beyond measure and we can embrace the moments of love that are available. Embracing moments of love will give you power, zeal, and energy.

Interestingly, there is even a biological component to love. Moments of love occur within the context of relationships and interactions where bonding takes place and the hormone oxytocin is released. Oxytocin has been nicknamed by some as the "cuddle hormone" or "love hormone." It acts within the body and the brain and plays a key role in social bonding and attachment. Although oxytocin is released during intercourse for both men and women and during childbirth and lactation for women, oxytocin is also released during everyday activities and interactions where bonding takes place—including playing with your children, meeting and getting to know new people, creating successful business deals with new partners, and hanging out with family and friends. Studies show oxytocin surges increase trust and cooperation. In other words, we are wired to love.

We often miss out on the opportunities to enjoy love connections of all types because they don't fit the mold of what we believe love should look like. I have experienced love during times of praise and worship and during prayer and meditation, both at church with others and alone in my prayer closet. I have also experienced these moments of love while playing with my grandchildren. Since I have become aware of the power of these moments of love, I experience them more deliberately and more often.

One of the reasons love is such a powerful force is that it cancels out negativity. Those who oppose and resist love often do so out of jealousy, envy, and the other issues with which many people struggle. Some who see you walking in love are immediately intimidated and confronted by their own shortcomings; instead of applauding your process and progress, they try to hinder you. The only way to successfully deal with these "haters" is through love. When you determine you will not allow the poisons of unforgiveness, bitterness, hatred, and resentment to enter your life and heart, you can continue in your love walk. I've found that praying for those who are against you while distancing them so they cannot hurt you are two surefire ways to love your enemies. Love is a healing force that keeps me on my knees.

And that brings me to the next pearl of wisdom—the power of prayer.

THE POWER OF PRAYER

I believe in the power of prayer. I have seen God move mightily because of prayer. Prayer allows you to communicate with—to actually talk with—God. And I assure you God loves to talk to his children.

I learned a secret of the universe when I learned how to pray. I can truly say I believe even more in the power of prayer today than I did then, because without prayer I would have no hope. Prayer is like oxygen to my hope—it keeps my hope alive.

Prayer is the first point of entry into transformation. When you begin to acknowledge that there is help available to strengthen you, your life will change. That's what happened to me when I started on my journey of hope.

People often begin prayers by asking God if he is there. I knew God existed. I knew him before I knew me. I always had a sense of God's presence. As a child, I often wandered away from home (in my high-crime neighborhood, no less!) as my thoughts focused on God. My parents frantically drove up and down the streets looking for me. It reminds me of the account in the Bible when Jesus got separated from Mary and Joseph and they found him teaching in the temple. I wasn't found in the temple, but I was being wooed by God, who would later fully introduce himself to me. And just like Mary, each time my parents found me, my mother scolded me for walking off. However, unlike Mary, she would pull me by the ear into the car and say, "Gal, don't you know better than to roam the neighborhood like that? You could be killed!" And I cried because I did not know how to put into words what I was feeling inside.

As an adult, I did not have to be convinced God was real; I just had to surrender my will to him. I'm so glad I did, because once I accepted Jesus, I began to have conversations with him about my life. I made a covenant with the Lord that I would tell him everything I was feeling and thinking, no matter how bad or crazy it was, because he already knew anyway. I loved walking and roller blading on park trails, spending time at beaches and lakes, and otherwise being alone in nature so that I could talk with God and tell him how I was struggling and how much I needed him. I still do that to this day, and our covenant is still very much in place. I walk and I talk with my best friend, who happens to be El Shaddai, or God Almighty.

After forming MIC, I also learned the power of intercessory prayer as I gathered my team together to pray for one another and for others. I believe that intercessory prayer is the highest form of prayer because it's not about you but about bridging the gap for others. As I pray for others, it brings me hope for their situation because I have placed them in the hands of Someone who loves them more than I ever could, Someone who can really help them. The hard part is leaving them there and not trying to carry their burdens on my incapable shoulders.

In addition to intercessory prayer, what really increased my hope is spiritual warfare prayer that includes fasting. I always say, "If you pray, you will stay, and if you fast, you will last!" Because of the deliverance that others and I received and because I realized that there are powers that resist change, I began to study deliverance ministry. In the 1990s, I traveled to Colorado to attend conferences with Peter and Doris Wagner at the World Prayer Center. These experiences revolutionized my prayer life as I learned how to "submit . . . to God [and] resist the devil" so that "he [would] flee" (James 4:7, NIV).

I have so many amazing stories about the power of prayer that I could write a whole book—and maybe one day I will. For now, I will share the behind-the-scenes story of what took place before the South African Hope Tour (see chapter 19). This incident wasn't as revolutionary as God giving me my mind back and delivering me from drugs, but it shows how everyday prayer infused with hope can result in miracles. Over the years I have learned that God is concerned about everything that concerns us; nothing is too small to take to the Lord in prayer, and nothing is too hard for him to answer.

As I shared earlier, four people traveled to South Africa with me: Kwame, Dr. Brenda "B. J." Jarmon, Sharon Durham, and Aaronetta Frison. We planned for our South African Hope Tour approximately six months in advance, coordinating the purchase of the airline tickets and working with Jonathan Annipen, our host coordinator in Durban, to make sure all the speaking and hotel arrangements were in place.

We encountered several complications that required us to pray for help. First, even though Dr. B. J. had expedited the process of renewing her passport months earlier, she still had not received it. She had called the US Department of State, and they were trying to help her, but we were scheduled to leave on a Sunday, and by Friday, she still did not have the passport. We began to pray especially hard concerning the obstacles standing in the way of her ability to travel with us. In the meantime, the rest of us were packed and ready to go.

Then the morning before we were to leave, Kwame woke me with some very disturbing news. I will never forget it. I opened my eyes and smiled up at him, but I noticed that he looked crestfallen. I sat up in the bed and asked, "What's happening, dear?"

"I've just checked my passport, and it's expired," he said.

I immediately jumped out of the bed and said, "Say that again, please, because I don't think I heard you correctly."

Kwame repeated the fact that his passport was expired. I immediately began to pray and to walk very softly for about fifteen minutes, and then I said these critical words of hope: "It's going to be all right." I can't explain how, but I was given peace and hope. I did know that we didn't have time to play the blame game and argue, which so often happens in cases like these. Instead, Kwame and I prayed together; as our faith connected, we found solutions.

Because it was Saturday, it was a challenge to talk to the right people, but while Kwame made calls to the State Department and to our airline, I called my prayer team from TPIC, and we had group prayer. Then we learned that Kwame could fly from Tallahassee to Atlanta (part of our originally scheduled flight), get his passport renewed, and then fly out on Monday—and Dr. B. J. could pick up her passport in Atlanta as well! It took a lot of praying and maneuvering, but the next day, the entire team flew from Tallahassee to Atlanta as planned. While the rest of us went on to South Africa, Kwame and Dr. B. J. spent the night in Atlanta, picked up their passports Monday morning, and left for South Africa later that day. They arrived a day after the rest of us, but we were just happy that they could both come.

THE POWER OF RESILIENCE

Resilience is essentially elasticity—the power or ability to return to the original form or position after being bent, compressed, or stretched. It is the ability to bounce back. I wish I could bottle resiliency and sell it; I would be a billionaire. Unfortunately, resiliency can't be bought, but it can be taught, and I was fascinated to learn that studies reveal that hope increases resiliency. Through the power of hope, resilience can be instilled in a person or group of people who are hopeless and feel that life is not worth living. I have seen it happen time and time again. Over the years, I've met women who have bounced back from horrendous, destructive situations, such as childhood sexual abuse, domestic violence, rape, single parenting five or more children, extreme poverty, mental illness, and drug addiction. The key ingredient in the recovery of each of these women was resilience.

I know how powerful and critical resilience is because it took resilience for me to go through the things I went through and not give up. Several years ago, I was able to make the connection between resilience and my ability to bounce back during my addiction after speaking to a sweet group of elderly ladies who belonged to a United Methodist Church women's auxiliary. After I finished telling them about my story of hope and MIC, one of the women, with tears in her eyes, asked me, "How in the world were you able to stay in school through all of the drug use and still finish college at Florida State University?" I looked at her and said, "It was the grace of God."

Later that night I began to think about her question, and I allowed myself to reflect on those days and try to remember how and what I was thinking. I asked myself what was motivating me to continue while many of my friends had flunked out and returned home. That reflection brought some insights.

Even when I had almost gotten kicked out of Florida State because of my grades, I had immediately gotten back in by changing my major from communications to social work. When I had had psychotic breaks with reality as a result of my drug abuse, I withdrew from college so I would still be in good standing when I came back. When I was in a mental institution for the last time, I told the staff there I was going to return to Florida State in the fall, and I did. I remembered that at the height of my addiction, I had consistently gotten up, gone to class, taken tests, and written papers. I had stayed in school when I had gotten in trouble with the law and been placed on probation; I had even stayed in school while I was homeless and had nowhere to lay my head.

After thinking about these things, I realized that getting a good education had been instilled in me—and no matter what I was going through, I knew I needed to graduate from college. Failing to graduate was not an option. All my immediate family members had gone to college, and they were all teachers. All my life, I had been told I would go to college, and I believe that graduating from college was important to me because my family valued education as a way out and up. Education represented hope for the future.

What you tell your children about their destiny is important. If you tell them they are not going to amount to anything in life, then nine times out of ten, that's what will happen. Parents have the awesome power to greatly impact their children, whether it is negative or positive. As parents, we need to make sure we speak about and instill good values that stick. We cannot expect schools, the government, or even churches to do it alone. We must be the first to do it. As parents and leaders, we have the responsibility to help our children and others develop the will to achieve and overcome, not just to survive. A true leader can inspire and motivate resilience in others by helping them find their places of hope. We become resilient and teach resilience when we remember that it's not how many times you fall but how many times you get back up that really counts.

THE POWER OF UNITY

Hope is needed for unity to survive, because hope is a unifying, non-sectarian force that is not based on social status, race, gender, political affiliation, or anything else. We all need hope in order to live. As a matter of fact, according to the oft-cited "survival rules of three," people can survive three weeks without food, three days without water, three hours without shelter, and three minutes without air, but only three seconds without hope.

When we come together in agreement around a cause, we become unstoppable because the power of unity changes people, families, communities, and nations. Together we can accomplish what we never could alone. An example of this—for good and bad—is found in Genesis 11, when the people of the world came together to build a tower that reached the heavens. They were unified in their (sinful) hope of building the tower. When God looked down and saw what they were doing and how successful they were, he confused their language so that they could no longer understand one another. No longer able to communicate, they lost hope and stopped building.

This scriptural account paints a powerful picture for us of the importance of clear communication and understanding when it comes to unity, because speaking the same language brings unity. We all speak certain languages, and I'm not just talking about English, Spanish, Swahili, Arabic, French, and so on. I'm referring to the jargon we speak in different professions and to the lingo of different cultures. Even churches have their own platitudes, such as "I'm blessed and highly favored" or "God is good all the time, and all the time, God is good." When we speak these lingos, jargons, and platitudes, we understand one another, and that understanding creates unity among us.

I learned about true unity and teamwork through my experiences in establishing MIC. I knew I couldn't do it by myself and that for the organization to be successful, it was going to take a group of like-minded individuals working together for the same goal. Over the years, one of the things I learned is that a powerful team cannot have hidden agendas—motives that are primarily selfish but are camouflaged to look like unity. When that happens, the team will implode from the inside out. I have found that good teams produce great leaders who are motivated by service.

I'm not saying members must be exactly alike for a team to be powerful, because God made us all different. The power comes when we put aside our differences and come together with a common goal of fulfilling a mission and vision. We all have different strengths and weaknesses, and we are only as strong as our weakest link. As a team, then, we must cover each other in prayer and support. It's not about comparing, competing, or fighting with each other; it's about coming together to fight against the enemy while accomplishing our goals.

Over the years, I have grown to appreciate the power that is in the unity of the Spirit that produces the bond of peace. I immensely enjoy working with the Christ Vision Tribe, Hope Squad, and Citizens of Hope of MIC as we display unity and singleness of mind. Our faith, passion to help others, commitment, honesty, and loyalty are the ingredients that make for a successful mission. We are united in hope, period—there is no other agenda and no other motive. As a result, we work together through thick and thin. This has helped keep us together in times of conflict. The glue that holds the team together in difficult times is the Holy Spirit. I thank God I am part of a group of people whose destinies are intertwined to productively live out our purposes while advancing the kingdom of God.

THE POWER OF HUMILITY

Humility is the modest sense of one's own importance, rank, and place in life. It's having a correct estimation of who you are and choosing to lift others higher than yourself through service in love. Humility is birthed when one surrenders her or his will to the will of God. There is true power in humility when it is mixed with hope, because hope says, "Weeping may endure for a night, but joy cometh in the morning" (Psalm 30:5, KJV).

People often mistake my meekness for weakness because I choose to walk humbly. I'm not a doormat for people to walk over; I have just learned that there is power in humility when I remain hopeful through the things I suffer, just as Jesus did when he humbled himself by becoming obedient to death on the cross. In Philippians 2:5, the bible states we are to have the same mindset—and we can when we know, as Jesus knew, that God the Father will exalt us.

The Bible also says Jesus learned obedience through the things he suffered (see Hebrews 5:8). I am convinced that suffering is designed to produce humility. I learned many things through suffering that I couldn't have learned any other way because of my stubborn and rebellious attitude.

I believe that addiction to drugs and alcohol is an act of rebellion that produces a mindset of selfishness. In order to break through the denial and negative thinking surrounding addiction, one must sometimes hit what is known as "bottom." Bottom is a place of suffering that in the best-case scenario produces surrender. Unfortunately, suffering can also produce hardness of heart if it is not received properly. I have met many people who seem to be in bottomless pits. No matter how hard they fall, they seem to have such tolerance for suffering that they continue doing things that produce more and more pain.

People like this have what I call spiritual leprosy. Leprosy, or Hansen's disease, causes the inability to feel pain in the infected part of the body. That may seem like a good thing, but because patients can't feel pain, they find it difficult to protect themselves from injury and even the loss of limbs. Similarly, people with spiritual leprosy have lost their ability to feel spiritual pain and have therefore lost their ability to spiritually protect themselves. As a result, they experience the loss of relationships, jobs, self-esteem, mind, freedom, and sometimes even life.

At the height of my addiction, I was one of those people with a high tolerance for suffering. I believe it stemmed from my ability to self-medicate and thus numb the pain of my early sexual abuse at the hands of my alcoholic uncle. The abuse started when I was five years old as he bounced me up and down on his lap, rubbing me against his penis. On one occasion, he even exposed himself to me and tried to have intercourse with me. I remember how terrified I felt; I ran out of the house and down the street, crying. I never told my parents or anyone what my uncle had done because I thought it was my fault. He used to give me candy and money before he fondled me; I thought that because I took the gifts, I was as guilty as he was. I learned much later that it didn't matter: I was a child and he was a grown man!

I didn't allow myself to tap into the feelings surrounding that violation and loss of innocence until I had lost my mind, my first child, and the love of my life and was facing the possible loss of another child. It took all of that for me to finally embrace the suffering that had always been a big part of my life. By embracing the suffering, I allowed myself to feel the pain without medicating. I allowed myself to cry and, most importantly, I allowed myself to cry out to God.

For me, embracing the suffering allowed me to embrace the One who suffered so much at the hand of humanity. I found that through getting to know Jesus the Christ—the One the Bible describes as being "a man of sorrows, acquainted with deepest grief" (Isaiah 53:3, New Living Translation, hereafter NLT)—I had someone who would be right there with me, who could relate to the pain I was experiencing, and who could help me in the process of surrender that led to my humility.

In order to truly surrender, I had to realize that it wasn't all about me. I subconsciously believed that by being rebellious and using drugs, I was getting back at my family for letting me down—more specifically, I was getting back at my mother for not protecting me from the abuse. I had to learn that even though I had been violated, life didn't revolve around me.

During the process of surrender, I became open to listening to others. I allowed the Holy Spirit to comfort me and heal me from the violation, guilt, and shame that I felt as a result of being sexually abused. Today I am free to feel! Whether the feelings are positive or negative, they are mine, and I am responsible for what I do with them. Today I can truly say that I choose to humble myself under the mighty hand of God, and he continues to lift me up time and time again through his love.

I also had to learn the difference between true humility and false humility. Sometimes people put on a façade of being humble when what they are really experiencing is low self-esteem and lack of self-worth. They believe they aren't valuable and that their experiences define who they are. Their self-talk is condemning, and they walk around with their heads hung low. Oftentimes they allow others to abuse them because they really believe they are "lower than a snake's belly." Essentially, they have no hope. But true humility is based on hope. When you really believe that God is for you and will exalt you in due time, you can have hope for the future. You can also know that your self-worth is defined by who you are as a child of God, not by what you have done.

When you are truly humble, you don't have to walk in pride and arrogance, demanding others notice and acknowledge you. You know who you are in Christ, and that is enough. Others may shun you or choose to try to put you down, but your humility will not allow them to, because you are already safe and secure in the arms of Abba (Father), and there is no better place to be. In Isaiah 57:15, the Bible says that God dwells with and revives those who are humble. God's abiding presence is where the true power of humility comes from.

THE POWER OF PASSION

The sufferings of Jesus Christ between the Last Supper and his death are called the Passion of Christ. Its power lies in the reason he chose to die for our sins. It took profoundly strong and abiding emotion to go through the Crucifixion on behalf of humanity. It took love. I am reminded of the account in Luke 7 about the woman who washed Jesus's feet with her tears and wiped them with her hair. Jesus said that the woman loved much because she had been forgiven much (see Luke 7:47, NIV).

I can relate to that woman in the Bible. I have given my all to the Lord and to help others because of what God did and continues to do for me. For me, passion is love in action, and I am a passionate person. Sometimes it is not expressed or shown on the outside as much as on the inside. Over the years, I've had to learn how to live as a passionate person in environments that do not appreciate or understand passion. I've even had to leave some organizations because I knew my passion for a cause was greater than that of others' and caused too many problems.

There is power in passion when it is mixed with hope, because passion can propel you into greatness or destruction, depending on how it is expressed. With hopeful passion, you really believe that what you are doing will make a difference—that you can change the world. Hopeful passion moves you to do something. It is not dormant. It's like fire; it spreads. It's like water; it flows. Hopeful passion is what keeps me moving forward in life.

Hopeful passion is the opposite of angry passion, which causes you to desire revenge against those who have hurt you or others. Angry passion drives you to destruction, while hopeful passion propels you to restoration. Even if passion starts out angry, it needs to be redirected into positive emotion in order to truly make a difference.

Drugs and alcohol numb one's ability to feel pain, but they awaken the ability to feel passionately about getting high. Addicts will do whatever it takes to get the drug; an addict, then, is a very passionate person. The only problem is that the passion is misguided. When I was addicted, I gave drugs and alcohol my all. I was driven by the addiction to get high every day. My whole life was centered on drug-using and drug-seeking behaviors.

When I began my journey to freedom, I found that I experienced life at a very deep level of love, joy, and pain, and I no longer felt the need to stuff my feelings out of sight. It's good to feel and express feelings, and there is no compassion without passion. In order to feel the hurt of others enough to be moved to help, one must be in touch with one's own feelings.

It is difficult to turn passion on and off. The very thing that makes me powerful in my ability to reach out and help others is the thing that is often attacked by a system designed around conformity. Over the years, I have faced situations where I've been told, "Don't take it personally," and "Don't make any waves." Telling a passionate person such things is like saying, "Don't breathe." One must breathe to live—and that's how I feel about passion. My passion is an intricate part of who I am, and if I kill the passion, part of me dies.

Some people express their passion through worldly desires, but we can all move toward higher goals designed to not only benefit ourselves but to help others along the way. There are a multitude of causes that need passionate people who are not intimidated by those with little or no passion. There is poverty in every city, state, country, and nation in the world. There are children and elderly being abused, and there are people dying who have never been loved. There are children growing up in homes with no father and sometimes no mother. Mental illness, homelessness, and addiction run rampant in our communities.

My passion is currently directed toward the Whole Hope Campaign, which I discuss in the next chapter. I am continuously enthused and excited about telling my story, empowering others to share their stories, and spreading hope to those who need it.

THE POWER OF YOU

In a day and age where society seems to be obsessed with superheroes who possess extraordinary powers—strength, speed, insight, and so on—it's important to know what makes you special. I believe everyone has a superpower—the "power of you."

There is no one else in the world like you, and what you contribute and bring to your life experience is valuable. When you don't know who you are, you cannot comprehend your worth. I have seen many women stay in abusive relationships because they don't know who they are, so they don't realize their self-worth. They believe they deserve to be hit, slapped, or cursed at. One of the greatest challenges is helping people know that they always deserve to be treated with respect and dignity, no matter what they have done or are doing. God created us all equal; that is how we should treat others and how we should be treated.

We often spend years imitating others while never quite knowing who we are. Knowing who you are and why you are here is the power you have to change the world. It starts with being and becoming, not just doing. Too often we identify ourselves by what we do instead of who we are. That's why it's important to know who you are, because there are no formulas or quick fixes in this life. You cannot just do certain things and figure that life will work out in certain ways. Life is messy, and there are lots of variables. Knowing who you are helps you navigate them all.

After all that has been said and done over the years, I know who I am and Whose I am! That knowledge has helped me through many challenging situations and has greatly assisted in my ability to help others know who they are. My self-discovery began once I entered recovery. In order to deal with esteem issues successfully, I had to first discover who I was, and I was delighted to learn that my behavior did not define me. I came to understand that I am a human being and not a human doing.

I also learned I couldn't let others define me and that I could not find my identity by imitating those I admired. I tried all that, and I still didn't have a clue as to who I really was. I finally ascertained that there is only One who can define me, and that is the One who made me. I found my identity when I found the Lord. Through his Word, I was able to see who I am in Christ, and by his Holy Spirit, I can walk in the light of that revelation. I derive hope from knowing I am loved unconditionally by God and that I am valuable.

Once I understood my value, I began to love myself as God loved me, which is unconditionally. In order to do that, I had to respect myself and not allow anyone to disrespect me. I have learned that people will devalue you based on their perceptions of your worth. We often judge people based on our own experiences. For example, some people believe the saying "Once an addict, always an addict," and they will treat you accordingly. But just because someone believes a certain thing about me does not make it true. I do not have to prove myself to anyone, because I have already been approved of God.

When embracing the power of you, the first thing is to get to know who you are as a person. What are your strengths and weaknesses, your likes and dislikes? The next thing is to find your purpose. What are you supposed to be doing? I found the answer to these questions through my relationship with God. Once you find out who you are and what you're supposed to be doing, believe it and stand by it. Don't be moved by people or circumstances.

Don't get into a mindset of trying to convince people of your worth, because some people may not see you for who you are. If they don't see your value, you just have to move on. Those who are supposed to see and value you will, and they are the ones with whom you can have mutually loving and respectful relationships. Living in the power of you becomes possible through hope because hope illuminates your path in life and helps you believe in the power that you have inside to make things better.

CONCLUSION

These eight pearls of wisdom are by no means exhaustive. There are many more principles by which I live, but these have continually influenced my life in deep and lasting ways. I am convinced that the things we go through in life are designed to prepare us for our purpose and destiny. Instead of regret for the things I've suffered, I am grateful for the way they helped shape me into the person I am today and the person I will become tomorrow. My journey of hope is by no means over. It has only just begun.

21

Releasing the Power of Hope

If I had to summarize everything I have gone through in life, I would have to say that having hope amid many difficult and challenging situations literally saved me. And I've seen hope save thousands of others, which is why MIC is conducting the Whole Hope Campaign to release the power of hope. An important part of this campaign is Hopeologist services. I trademarked the term *Hopeologist* with the US Patent and Trademark Office; it is defined as "Promoting public awareness of hope by means of public advocacy." Hopeologist services consist of promoting Fridays as Hope Universe Day and April as the National Month of Hope.

My hope work includes hope coaching, podcasts, blogs, trainings, seminars, summits, and workshops, all designed to share practical ways for people and society in general to practice hope by becoming more hopeful. Utilizing components of social, spiritual, and educational models, MIC advocates for hope as a way of thinking and living.

Radio tours are one of the vehicles we use to make the public aware of the Whole Hope Campaign. We conducted our first radio tour during the inaugural National Month of Hope in April 2018. Since that time, I have been interviewed on countless radio shows across America, spreading the message of hope. One of the key things I talk about is the fact that America is facing a hope crisis. A major indicator of the hope crisis is the increase in the suicide rate; according to the Center for Disease Control and Prevention, the suicide rate among the US working age population increased 34 percent from 2000–2016. We continue to hear about the suicides of high-profile celebrities who appear to have it all. I believe suicide is increasing because Americans are in despair, and many psychological, biological, societal, and social factors are contributing to that despair. Some of the major crises include the increase in untreated mental illness, the opioid epidemic, the divisiveness of the political climate, gun violence (including school shootings), major natural disasters, domestic violence, systemic racism, and poverty, to name a few. These issues paint a very pessimistic picture.

The good news is that there is still hope, and through the Whole Hope Campaign, we can turn this around one person at a time. People across the United States are learning about the Whole Hope Campaign and realizing that hope is exactly what this nation needs. Some think a movement toward hope is nothing more than wishful or positive thinking. But I know firsthand how the power of hope can and does change lives, starting with my own.

I now want to share powerful, practical concepts that will enable you to wrap your head, hands, and heart around hope. I truly believe that if each person does these things and helps others to do them, the world will be a better place. I challenge everyone to think hope, make hope connections, take hope breaks, and rest in hope.

THINK HOPE

Hope is defined as the expectation that something good will occur. As part of the Whole Hope Campaign, we are encouraging everyone to "think hope."

When you think hope, you look for the good in every challenging situation. When you think hope, you believe things can and will get better. When you think hope, you can find solutions because hope is like a light shining in a dark tunnel. The light of hope illuminates your path.

It sounds simple, but it's actually quite difficult to think hope. It's easier to let your thoughts roam wherever they want to go, which is often to a negative place. However, it is worth the effort to think hope instead of negativity, because studies reveal that hopeful people excel in life, live longer, and live well.

People often say that thinking hope doesn't work and that it's Pollyanna-ish thinking. I have found that it *does* work to think hope, because I've seen how my life and the lives of others have been tremendously transformed through the power of hope. It's not always easy, but it is doable and worth it to think hope.

Some object to this idea by saying, "What if I think hope but things never change or get better?" The best thing about thinking hope is that even if things don't change, *you* change. Suddenly, what you thought was failure becomes possibility because hope brings purpose and encourages you to stop asking "Why?" and start asking "Why not?" We are admonished in the Bible to think about what is true, honorable, right, pure, lovely, admirable, excellent, and worthy of praise (see Philippians 4:8, NLT). That sounds hopeful to me. Check out my Think Hope podcast by visiting www.blogtalkradio.com/thinkhope.

HOPE CONNECTIONS

As part of the Whole Hope Campaign, we are encouraging everyone not only to think hope but to make hope connections. A hope connection occurs when you bring hope to someone by connecting to them with your heart. This can occur through hope chats, hope fusions, and hope spheres.

With so much happening all around the nation and world, we could all use a little hope from time to time. A hope chat occurs when you bring hope through your conversation to someone who needs it. That person can be a family member, a coworker, a friend, or someone you meet while standing in line at the grocery store.

We are finding that hope chats are really making a difference in people's lives. One story that comes to mind is of a young man who came to

Nettie's house asking to mow the lawn. He told Nettie that his marriage was in trouble and he was looking for work. He and his wife had four children; he was tired of trying and failing, and he was at the end of his rope. Nettie had a hope chat with this young man, and he left her home hopeful for the first time in months.

Two weeks later, the young man stopped by Nettie's house to tell her that things had worked out for him. He had found a job, and his marriage was improving. He thanked her for taking the time to talk with him.

It's just that simple to let someone know you care. Doing so gives a person hope to try one more time.

Hope chats are an excellent way of both giving and receiving hope, because hope flows both ways. You cannot give hope without receiving more hope. I have experienced this on many occasions; as I give the gift of hope, more hope always comes back to me.

It's easy to have a successful hope chat if you follow these seven steps:

1. *Identify* someone who needs hope.
2. *Prepare* yourself for the conversation. Turn on your belief that things can get better, and put on your unconditional love.
3. Go to the person you've identified, look him or her in the eye, and say something like, "I care about you and wanted to check in with you to see how things are going."
4. As the person shares, listen with a "hope face." A hope face is open and warm, and it is created when you look at someone and really see and connect with him or her. It is kind, joyful, and nonjudgmental.
5. After the person finishes sharing, encourage him or her by saying something like, "I can understand why you might see things that way." Then ask, "Deep down, what do you want most?"

6. After listening to the person's answers, empower him or her by saying something like, "I have an idea of what you can do. May I share it with you?"

7. Wrap up by saying something like, "Just know that I am here for you and I believe that things are going to get better. Remember, as long as there is breath in your body, there is hope."

HOPE FUSIONS

Once you have made a hope connection by having a hope chat, you may find during the wrap-up step that you and the other person agree to meet on a consistent basis. At MIC, we call that a hope fusion because you are coming together and continuing to share hope.

Kwame experienced a hope fusion when he met with someone who was going through a rough time. The two of them decided to meet monthly, and it really made a difference in that person's ability to get back on his feet. He told Kwame that just having someone to talk with made a big difference. During the process, Kwame found that he received way more hope than he gave, because you cannot give without receiving.

Here are the five steps to a successful hope fusion:

1. After the hope chat, agree to have ongoing conversations to reinforce progress.
2. During subsequent conversations, share stories of hope with one another.
3. Connect with your hearts.
4. Continue to share words of encouragement.
5. Create bonds and mutually agreed upon outcomes.

HOPE SPHERES

A *hope sphere* is created when a group of people decides to create an atmosphere of hope in which each person begins to think hope, have hope chats, and participate in hope fusions. Hope spheres generally occur when a group of three or more people comes together in hope. In hope spheres, you cultivate hopeful environments filled with encouragement and love. Hopeful atmospheres can blossom within families, communities, cities, states, and nations when you create hope spheres in homes, businesses, religious institutions, and other organizations.

We practice what we preach at MIC, and we have created a hope sphere among ourselves where we intentionally practice hope. That hope sphere has radically changed the productivity and overall well-being among members of the group. The contrast between the early days of MIC and the current environment is like night and day. As just one example, there used to be a lot of backbiting and negative talk among the members and leaders of MIC. It created a lot of mistrust and drama. I'm happy to say that since we began to practice hope, we deal with conflict differently and there is no conflict now.

Our hope sphere is filled with the fruit of the Spirit that is identified in Galatians 5:22–23 as love, joy, peace, patience, kindness, goodness, faithfulness, gentleness, and self-control. As we think hope, we find solutions and anchor ourselves in hope. Although we are not always individually hopeful, the hopeful atmosphere helps. We also periodically check up on one another, and as a result, no one stays in a negative mindset for too long.

The motto of the state of Rhode Island is Hope, and there are countless cities, organizations, and communities that have the word *hope* in their names and mission statements. Imagine if everyone who identified with hope began to practice hope. Just considering that brings me hope!

Here are the five steps to creating successful hope spheres:

1. *Gather* families, groups, teams, companies, churches, or organizations for hope fusions.
2. *Share* stories of hope with one another.
3. *Connect* with your hearts.
4. *Pledge* to continue to share words of encouragement by having hope chats when needed.
5. *Create* hopeful environments.

HOPE BREAKS

When people ask how I stay hopeful amid so much turmoil, I usually start by explaining the importance of the company we keep. You cannot hang around negative people and remain hopeful. Hope chats also keep me hopeful. Another important factor is a practice we developed at MIC we call "taking hope breaks." Unless you schedule time to think hopeful thoughts, negativity and despair will creep up like thieves in the night.

When I find myself feeling down, nothing picks me up like a good hope break! Once I realized that, I started to schedule hope breaks throughout the day. During these breaks, I stop and intentionally think about good and hopeful things.

MIC is challenging everyone to take hope breaks throughout the day. Here are the steps to taking successful hope breaks:

1. *Schedule* hope breaks into your normal routine in five-minute increments.
2. *Find* a quiet place.
3. *Take* five to ten deep breaths.
4. *Think* about the good things that are happening; instead of entertaining worst-case scenarios, think of best-case scenarios.
5. *Make* an affirmation and speak it out loud.
6. Repeat as often as needed.

REST IN HOPE

Psalm 16:9 (KJV) states: "Therefore my heart is glad, and my glory rejoiceth: my flesh also shall rest in hope." I shared this scripture at one of our chapel services at TPIC and explored the meaning and importance of our bodies resting in hope while we are alive—because once we are dead, doing so will allow us to rest in peace.

It's often difficult to *rest* in hope because hope is an expectation of something good or better to happen, and that expectation creates an excitement that makes it hard to rest. It's similar to how, when I was a young child, I could not sleep at all the night before Christmas because I was so excited about opening all my presents. Sometimes I have felt that way since I have been practicing hope. It's as if every day is the night before Christmas, but now the excitement comes not from *what* I am expecting but rather from *Whom*. I am expecting God to be good, and I am never disappointed even when things don't go my way. We are told in the Bible, "And we know that in all things God works for the good of those who love him, who have been called according to his purpose" (Romans 8:28, NIV). So even if an experience is not good *to* me, it is good *for* me, and there is a life lesson to be learned.

Making up in your mind to live in hope can take a toll on your body if you are not careful. To rest in hope properly requires you to take care of your body. To rest is to relax from work and trust. When you rest in hope, you trust that God is with you and that everything will work out fine.

Here are seven ways to rest in hope:

1. Cease from worry.
2. Learn to eat nutritiously, move your body daily, and breathe correctly to calm yourself.
3. Meditate and pray.
4. Expect good things, and don't allow negativity to weigh you down.
5. Take it easy, slow down, pace yourself, and develop an appropriate life rhythm.
6. Focus on one task at a time.
7. Get proper sleep, take mini vacations, enjoy spa days, and take time off work.

MOVING FROM DESPAIR TO HOPE

I'm a HOPE (Helping Others Practice Empowerment) Life Coach, which means I coach people in finding and maintaining hope. Many of my clients are going through transitions because of loss—such as the loss of a loved one, a job, or a dream. Loss often breeds despair. However, I've found that hope is a powerful force that can take you through any trial or tribulation you may be facing.

I've shared my story of addiction and recovery and revealed how I have personally experienced loss on many levels throughout my life. After experiencing such loss, I can say with assurance that life is better with hope. Hope is like the knight in shining armor who comes just in time, right before you are about to give up, and says, "It may be hard right now, but hold on—tomorrow is coming, and things will get easier." And inevitably, things *do* get easier.

Here are seven steps to help you move from despair to hope:

1. Determine the cause of your despair. Be brutally honest; this requires self-evaluation and knowing that no one else is responsible for your feelings and emotions but you.
2. Confirm with someone you trust that you are on the right track in identifying the source of your despair.
3. Plan your strategy to move from despair to hope.
4. Set goals. See yourself completing your plan. Believe you can.
5. Focus on the result. Don't get distracted.
6. Pray and ask God for help.
7. Reach out to people who believe in your potential and who are willing to empower, not control, you along the way.

SYMBOLS OF HOPE

As part of the Whole Hope Campaign, we began administering the MIC Survey of Hope to random people in person and online during the National Month of Hope in April 2018. We've continued surveying people (some of whom agree to be video recorded as they answer the questions), and we always ask these four questions:

1. What is hope?
2. What brings you hope or makes you feel hopeful?
3. What are some things that zap your hope or make you feel less hope or hopeless?
4. What do you experience when you are hopeful?

Once we compile the data (which we are still doing as of this writing), we will share the results each year during the National Month of Hope. We will also choose programs and initiatives to support based upon our findings. Preliminary results reveal that most participants feel children bring hope. A high percentage of participants also feel that other people and their own faith in God bring them hope. Many people state that negativity and negative people zap their hope. When we ask about what people experience when they feel hopeful, answers vary from excitement and elation to peace and calm. Clearly, people experience hope in different ways.

HOPE SYMBOLISM

As we have been asking the survey questions, I have noticed how symbols of hope are very important to having and keeping hope. Universal symbols of hope are often subtle but can create a more hopeful environment. Based on our observations, we have compiled a list of symbols of hope; while this is by no means an exhaustive list, it demonstrates that there are symbols of hope all around.

> **Images:** cross, anchor, butterfly, rainbow, baby, hot-air balloon, star, Christmas, lighthouse, waterfall, candle, the sun, blue sky and white clouds, sunrise, sunset, the moon, smile, laughter, thumbs-up, high five, summer rain shower, ocean, mountains, bubbles
>
> **Birds:** doves (white and mourning)

Animal: dog
Number: four (4)
Flowers: sunflowers, daffodils, cactus flowers
Colors: yellow, green, red, blue, orange
Aromas: peppermint, lavender, vanilla, citrus
Sounds: ocean waves, wind chimes, waterfalls
Person: Jesus
Season: spring
Trees: pine, weeping willow, oak
Seeds: mustard, acorn

SPREADING HOPE

The MIC Hope Squad continues to spread and share hope every Friday (Hope Universe Day) and during the National Month of Hope (April). Here are some ways you can spread hope and make a difference:

- Volunteer by reading to children in schools.
- Support missions overseas.
- Give of your time, food, and money to help families in need in your community.
- Write letters to and visit those incarcerated.
- Post words of hope on social media.
- Have hope chats and share your story of overcoming with those going through hard times.
- Lend a helping hand to those in need.
- Cook a meal or going to the grocery store for the elderly.
- Clean up areas where there is trash, such as parks and beaches.
- Spend a day with the homeless, whether on the streets or in a shelter. Unless you walk a mile in their shoes, you won't know how to help them.

CITIZENS OF HOPE

An integral and significant part of our Whole Hope Campaign is the Citizens of Hope (COH) initiative. Citizens of Hope are individuals and organizations that support the Whole Hope Campaign financially on a monthly basis. COH are united in the belief that hope is a powerful force that helps people navigate challenging times. We believe we can have hope and spread hope to others, period. We have no other agenda or motives.

As we unite in hope, that hope shines light and reveals solutions. We are learning how to translate the abstract concept of hope into concrete actions through thinking hope, celebrating Hope Universe Day and the National Month of Hope, having hope chats, and taking hope breaks. As we come together with a perspective of hope, we focus on expectations of good outcomes instead of focusing on things that are divisive and destructive. Emphasizing our differences instead of our similarities zaps the power of hope. Hope's unifying force goes far beyond race, gender, political affiliation, religion, or social status. Despair may come naturally in times of personal and public crisis, but for COH, hope keeps us moving forward as we adopt a hopeful attitude.

We currently have several COH, and the number is increasing daily. Now I'd like to introduce you to three amazing individuals who have joined with MIC to support the hope agenda. They each share in their own words why they became COHs.

AARONETTA FRISON:
WHAT IT MEANS TO BE A CITIZEN OF HOPE

A citizen is someone registered to dwell in a certain location and a legally recognized resident of that locale. I am a Citizen of Hope—registered through PayPal to dwell there and legally recognized as a result of my close affiliation with Dr. Rosalind Y. Tompkins.

I became attached to Dr. Tompkins when my mother, the Rev. Dr. Bernyce Clausell, announced at a black-history program that Dr. Tompkins was her role model. I was going through some issues in life at the time, and hope dwelled in me. But after going through life coaching, mentorship, and seminary school with Dr. Tompkins, I now dwell in hope. I live there; hope is my home.

Being a citizen has its privileges. As a Citizen of Hope, I can browse the Hope Universe website at any time to keep abreast of events, resources, great hope thoughts, interviews, poetry, mission trips, and projects, among other things. Being a COH gives me access to Dr. Rosalind Tompkins for life coaching, counseling, hope chats, and prayer. As a citizen of hope, I am also kept up to date on Dr. Tompkins's speaking engagements, radio and TV interviews, podcasts, and broadcasts. Being a COH enables me to be empowered to help myself and others by spreading the message of hope one person at a time.

DR. BRENDA "B. J." JARMON: THOUGHTS ABOUT BEING A CITIZEN OF HOPE

Hope is the air we breathe; it is waking up in the morning; it is having faith in Jesus Christ and in his Word; it is stepping out in faith. While hope means different things to different people, I believe there are four common aspects to this thing called hope that should encourage COHs:

H: Honoring God gives us hope; his holiness gives us hope.

O: Opportunities to serve and obey God's Word give us hope.

P: Prayer, perseverance, patience, and purpose give us hope.

E: Engaging, empowering, enlightening, and evangelizing for and about our Lord gives us hope.

My children, grandchildren, and family give me hope. Above all, being a servant-leader and disciple for our Lord and Savior gives me hope and cements me as a COH.

Lord knows I have had my hope zapped by suffering from illness (a major surgery in 2013), experiencing two rear-end accidents (in 2007 and 2015), facing the deaths of my parents (in 2010 and 2016), and having two children by the time I was fifteen years old (in 1966 and 1967). I was a pregnant and parenting teen whose children's father left her high and dry, paid no child support, and ended up in jail for most of our children's lives. Added to all that stress and anxiety, I had no money, no job, no food for my children, and no transportation. All of it was enough to make the average person give up.

What kept me hopeful? Consider Proverbs 22:6 (KJV), which says, "Train up a child in the way he should go: and when he is old, he will not depart from it." Simply put, I was raised to be hopeful. I may have given up on myself, but none of the others who were important to me—my parents, my siblings, my grandparents, and a small group of folks in Selbyville, Delaware—gave up on me. Though most of the people in my hometown said I would amount to nothing, I was raised to never give up—especially to never give up on God! I was taught to turn negatives into positives. As a result, I found joy and peace in our Savior, which allowed hope to flow. I know now that I am covered in his blood, a condition that allows me to "have faith as small as a mustard seed" (Matthew 17:20, NIV).

As a COH, I can pay it forward and empower, motivate, and inspire others by sharing my testimony of the extremities from which God has brought me. I can be a servant who helps others build their hope and faith quotients through prayer, perseverance, patience, and purpose. *To God be the glory!*

MARGY OTIATO: A CASE FOR HOPE CITIZENSHIP

Every believer is wired with hope. It is our birthmark, our trademark as saints. We are designed to deal in hope as our core business in the process of believing and responding to the Great Commission.

Anyone who is stranded should look no further than to a believer who has encountered the living hope in Jesus Christ. Eternal value does not come from money, drugs, sex, work, food, or anything similar. A believer can be identified by how much hope he gives the people around him. While religion offers only limited benefits, we as believers provide a hope perspective and, as Christ's ambassadors who are filled with hope, we can change individuals and the world.

I have come to this greater realization through my journey of faith and through my ongoing encounters with Dr. Rosalind Tompkins and her unique ministry and brand of hope. Despite being a believer for many years, I have not arrived. I still have personal struggles that inhibit my fruitfulness, and Dr. Rosalind's testimony of how God delivered her from a hopeless way of life has boosted my faith. The new hope perspective I have gained from her is like the value attained from a newfound friendship. In life, we sometimes need just one word, one person with another spirit or perspective, to help shift our focus, to pull us out of the rut in which we're stuck, and to help us make the next leap forward. In these kinds of strategic partnerships, we can find a miraculous release into our true purpose.

My partnership with this ministry as a COH is giving me that privilege, push, and confidence at no cost. I feel certified and good to go in life just because of hope. I have come to appreciate that I need no longer wait for another move of God or another brand in the market in which to invest. No, all I need is in this hope movement. This is my "it"! Thank you, Dr. Rosalind, for extending this hope opportunity and the privileges that come with it.

To learn more about the Whole Hope Campaign and how you can become a COH, please visit www.makeahopeconnection.com.

22

Hope Thoughts and Poems of Hope

As we have discussed, what you think determines who you are—and your ability to think hope may require that you program or reprogram your mind. The Bible says, "For as he thinketh in his heart, so is he" (Proverbs 23:7, KJV), and we are counseled to think of things that are good and virtuous (see Philippians 4:8). In order to think hope, you must think about things that will fuel your faith and hope, which is why it is always beneficial to meditate on the Word of God.

Below are forty biblically based hope thoughts on which you can meditate. Ponder one of these thoughts each day for forty days to begin the process of rewiring your brain. Use the hope thoughts in conjunction with your hope breaks, and watch your hope level rise. You will find yourself smiling more while enjoying better overall health and well-being. As I shared earlier, studies reveal that hopeful people excel in life, live longer, and live well.

DAY 1	Laughter is the sound of hope.
DAY 2	If you are breathing, there is hope, because a live dog is better than a dead lion.

DAY 3	It's never too late; there is still hope.
DAY 4	May the God of hope fill you with joy and peace.
DAY 5	Expect great things to happen to you.
DAY 6	Find the hope; look for it, and it will appear.
DAY 7	Hope is like helium in your balloon of faith; let hope take you higher.
DAY 8	It takes only a spark of hope to illuminate your path and see that something better is on the way.
DAY 9	Watch out for hope killers.
DAY 10	Hope makes your heart sing.
DAY 11	Hope says, "It's worth the wait."
DAY 12	Hope is like ice cream for the soul.
DAY 13	Imagine a hopeful world.
DAY 14	Expect a miracle.
DAY 15	"Those who hope in the Lord will renew their strength. They will soar on wings like eagles" (Isaiah 40:31, NIV).
DAY 16	Hope is like the never-ending waves of the ocean.
DAY 17	Hope says, "Never give up."
DAY 18	Hope gives purpose, and purpose brings hope.
DAY 19	We walk by faith, and we run by hope.
DAY 20	May your tears water your garden of hope.
DAY 21	Hope is an anchor for your soul.
DAY 22	Hope says, "Let go of the past and look ahead."
DAY 23	Hope is the fresh air that blows away the cobwebs of despair.
DAY 24	Hope is like stars shining through the night; hope is the light turning darkness into day.
DAY 25	A leader is a dealer in hope.
DAY 26	Children are hope for our future.
DAY 27	Look for symbols of hope all around.
DAY 28	Something good is going to happen; receive it with gratitude.

DAY 29	Despair says "Not ever"; hope says, "Not yet, but it's coming."
DAY 30	Your choices make you great, so choose hope and live.
DAY 31	After all I have been through, I still have hope.
DAY 32	Since we rise to the level of our expectations, let hope raise the bar.
DAY 33	Faith moves mountains; hope moves people.
DAY 34	Celebrate hope today.
DAY 35	Live life from the place of expectation, excitedly, like Christmas every day.
DAY 36	We do not grieve as though we have no hope (see 1 Thessalonians 4:13).
DAY 37	There is unity in hope.
DAY 38	Keep trying.
DAY 39	Hope, like candles, needs fire to burn bright; keep hope burning.
DAY 40	Joy is the fruit of hope.

Over the years, I have found that poetry is an excellent way to express my feelings on a deep level. I've also seen the power of poetry bring hope to people who are going through tough times. Writing and reciting poetry has helped me think hope and stay in a place of positivity. It has saved my life on a few occasions when I was down and depressed. I would like to leave you with a few of my original poems. Some are new, and some are classics (at least to me), but they are all designed to bring hope.

STARDUST OF HOPE

Hope is like the stars shining through the darkness of night,
Providing light to navigate through tough times.
In the midst of the madness and mayhem, hope continues to shine as
*   I look up to the heavens.*

I'm looking at the substance God used to make man from his hand: stardust. In him I trust.

I see myself shining through the darkness of night, and I know that it will be all right because I see many shining brightly beside me.

Together, our chemistry forms a lighthouse of hope to help others find their way through the darkness of night.

We join hands and hope is our light, and we pray to turn the darkness into day.

AUTUMN'S HOPE

The leaves are falling one by one, leaving the safety and security of the trees.

I sneeze as I feel the chill while beholding the warmth of autumn's colors.

The browns, reds, oranges, rusts, golds, and evergreens are prominently seen.

The smells of cinnamon, pumpkin, peppermint, and spice permeate the atmosphere and make nice aromatherapy.

It brings me clarity, and I know that just as the leaves leave the trees, I too must shed last season's skin and begin again.

It's time to store up all the good things God brings.

Sitting by the fireplace sipping tea with a warm blanket surrounding me,

I'm filled with peace, love, and joy while anticipating what's going to be,

Listening, writing, meditating, hibernating, and awaiting the birth of hope.

April, the month that's been set aside to breathe new life into things that have died—a whole month of hope, time to open wide the door of expectancy.

In the meantime, I enjoy autumn and its slower pace because it is
here that I receive the grace through the beautiful colors and
warm embrace
As the leaves leave the trees and I shed last season's skin to begin again.

WHERE IS HOPE?

Hope is found in the breath I breathe,
In the stars in the sky and the cool of the breeze.
Hope is found in a baby's cry or tears rolling down the eye
Of one who knows that every good thing flows from the heart of God.
Hope is found in the birds that sing, in the grass as it grows,
In the smell of a rose, in the dew as it settles upon the ground.
Hope can be found in the middle of pain, in the streets of frustration,
And in the home of the Name that is above every name!
Hope is found when you hear the Name, think the Name, or say
the Name.
It's all the same
Because Jesus is hope!

TODAY, I LISTEN

Today, I listen. I sit at his feet, and I listen.
I don't say a word. The only voice that will be heard
Is the voice of my Lord and Savior.
Today, I listen. I sit at his feet, and I listen.
I turn off the noise from inside and out.
I won't be distracted or worried about anything.
Listening is about quieting the heart, choosing the good part
Right from the start of the day.
Abba, Father, wants to take me away, to the isle of Patmos, the
Gardens of
Eden and Gethsemane, the mountains of Hermon and Sinai,
To the places where I try to hear the Holy Spirit's cry as I die to my flesh.

My spirit is refreshed and renewed in his presence.

I feel the essence of his love as I watch and wait.

Suddenly tears start to flow, and I know that my love has come.

Today, I listen. I sit at his feet, and I listen.

HOPE, WAKE US FROM THIS NIGHTMARE

Madness and mayhem in the wake of a massacre,

Leaving people wondering what is happening.

The political pundits saying it's about gun control and banning all Muslims,

Religious fanatics saying its God's judgment,

ISIS taking credit.

Children confused,

People looking for answers.

Orlando, the place where dreams come true—not you too.

Hope, wake us from this nightmare.

Tell us that tomorrow will be a better day.

Tell us that politics will cease and the violence will end.

Tell us that the hatred will die and that terror can't win.

Hope, wake us from this nightmare and let the light of love shine through.

Chase away the darkness and help us see our way to the land of promise where dreams do come true.

Hope, wake us from this nightmare and stop the mindless chatter— because lives have been taken, and all lives do matter.

SOUTH AFRICA PROUD

Note: The rand is the currency used in South Africa.

When I traveled to the continent of Africa thrice and in South Africa twice,

I learned the rhythm of the Spirit, the power of God. I can still hear it, deep in my heart, and I can feel it.

The openness of those who are near it makes me proud!

Proud to be a servant of the Most High, willing to fight and not afraid to die for the Lord,

Proud to be in the family of Christ, joined with others who are Spirit-nice, loving the Lord and on one accord.

From Richards Bay to Durban and then Cape Town, we experienced the explosion and heard the sound of God's remnant preparing for the big showdown soon to come,

The time when our Lord comes back again to gather his bride to be by his side forever and ever.

Until then, we wait and congregate as we expand the kingdom of God.

South Africa, South Africa, keep your finger on the pulse of the things that matter. No matter how it appears, just remember that you are set free by Jesus Christ, and whom the Son sets free is free for life.

So there is no need to fear or fret. The God we serve will never forget the love and kindness you bestowed. The half of it has not been told. As you seek, you will find it's more precious than gold.

From the bishops, the pastors, the apostles, the evangelists, the psalmists, the musicians, the servants, the members, the women, the children, the families, the gentlemen, the churches, the schools, the youth programs, the radio stations, the hotels and the homes, the cooked meals, the restaurants, the malls, the gifts, and the rands—in sickness and in health, God was in command. And the glory of the Lord filled every woman and man: casting out devils, healing the sick, saving souls, cleansing, and making whole.

South Africa, South Africa, you have found your It,

So stay in the Lord and never quit.

Remain under the glory cloud, South Africa proud!

"YES, LORD"

Jesus sees, and he knows the struggle, the pain, and the shame in claiming the Name that is above all names.

He sees your anguish and hears your cry as you wonder why it has to be this way.

But just as many who came before you believed in a brighter day, another way to live, and say that Jesus is the way, the truth, and the light,

You too must fight the good fight of faith as you wait and meditate on God's Word.

May his peace, love, and grace fill the place, with his glory resting on each face as you praise him and run the race set before you.

Also know that your brothers and sisters are standing with you, praying and believing for you to do well because the gates of hell will not prevail against you!

Turkey, Turkey, a gathering place for the broken and wounded souls fleeing for their lives, refugees on their knees, praying for relief:

God sees, and he knows, and he says to those who will go, "Feed my sheep and be restored," and we say, "Yes, Lord!"

TODAY I DIE AGAIN

I came to the Congo and received just what I thought I would. Sometimes I believe I look for the good in the midst of the bad—oh, so sad—but I'm actually glad I have prayed and prepared for what is to inevitably come. Sometimes I feel dumb, lost for words, and the stinging is felt and heard in the chambers of my heart.

I pray now for peace and true release from the grip of the hole. Please fill now, oh, Lord, with the gold of oil, precious and bold, balm for my soul.

Oh, how I trust You, dear Lord. You have always been there for me, and You continue to set me free. Please touch me now, oh, Lord, where I hurt. Remove the dirt and wash the wound with

frankincense and myrrh so the smell that emerges of burning
flesh will be a sweet-smelling sacrifice You have blessed, accept-
able and holy for the Master's use.
Okay, now it's getting better. "Ahhh," I sigh while wondering why it
has to be this way day after day into months and years, through
smiles painted on and tears that well up and spill over.
Tears our God bottles up for the years to come, to become the overflow,
for others to know and be delivered from sin—
For today, "I die again!"

WHAT DOES REJECTION TASTE LIKE?

What does rejection taste like?
The women in Congo who have been raped and rejected, they know
the taste.
I do too—it's neither sweet nor salty.
It's not sour or spicy. It's more like so bland you can't stand the taste.
It's the taste of void and emptiness,
A taste that is nothing, nothing, nothing.
That's what rejection feels like: nothing, like I'm nothing!
Oh, taste and see that the Lord is good.
The taste of Jesus is sweeter than honey on a honeycomb.
It's the only taste that can remove the taste of rejection:
Love, love, love.
That's what Jesus feels like: love, like I'm accepted in the beloved.
In Congo I found honey—in a place you wouldn't expect to find it,
just as Sampson found honey in the carcass of a lion.

PIGS IN THE SHADOWS

Haiti, dear lady-in-waiting, waiting for your breakthrough to come,
when justice is finally done and you receive recompense for the
grave offense that has been waged against you by the forces of
darkness.

*The pigs in the shadows will no longer be, and you will be free to live
life abundantly.*

*Haiti, dear lady, your waiting is not in vain. You won't even remem-
ber the pain when your Redeemer rises and says, "Enough!"*

*Enough of the poverty—you will receive prosperity. Enough of the
sickness and disease—you will now receive beauty for ashes and
the oil of joy for mourning. No more pigs in the shadows, because
Christ died for you, and by his crimson blood and unconditional
love, you will make it through. Because you have been redeemed
from the curse, and he makes all things new, hallelujah!*

*Haiti, dear lady-in-waiting, you shall give birth to purpose. So stop
the stalling, because you have many children destined to fulfill
their calling. No more pigs in the shadows—you will know what
really matters as you are transformed into the image of Christ.*

IN THE MIDST OF IT ALL

As you live your life, going through trials and tests,
There are some things that can cause you great stress.
They come to make you want to give up;
They zap your energy and empty your cup.
But in the midst of it all, you can stand tall!
In the midst of it all, on him you must call.
He will hear and answer your cry.
Why don't you just try?
Even if you have had a fall,
He is right there with you in the midst of it all,
Waiting on your call.
*Call on Jesus. Don't be like King Saul, who went to the witch and
dug a great ditch into which he did fall!*
*Seek the Lord. Give him a call because he is right there with you in
the midst of it all!*

DESTINY IS FULFILLED

The time has come, and the time is now.
You have been looking and searching because you didn't know how
*   you were going to make it; you just couldn't take it.*
The trials and tribulations of life got you down.
It got so bad until you thought you would drown in your own blood;
*   but like a flood, the Spirit lifted up a standard and brought you*
*   through it.*
Although you couldn't see it, you made it to it—the place of destiny.
You heard the call and had to dream again after the fall because,
*   after all, you believed inside that you are more than your prob-*
*   lems and more than your pain.*
You are much more than that; but all the same, you had to know and
*   do the Father's will because that is the way destiny is fulfilled!*
Who you are is who you shall be; your purpose in life lies within.
Deep inside, you see you can win because greatness is there and that
*   is who you are.*
When you trust in Jesus, then you can go far—high above the clouds
*   and sit upon a star—and look down over your problems and*
*   say, "Peace, be still,*
Because from where I'm sitting, destiny is fulfilled!"

DREAM AGAIN

I had a dream last night, but it didn't last long.
In the dream, I was singing a song
About how in life things can go wrong,
But even then, there is a chance to go on.
I had a dream last night about what love looked like,
And in the dream, I thought about the plight of men and women
Caught up in a daze, purple haze, eyes all glazed, looking half crazed,
Walking and wandering through life unfazed by all the chaos and
*   sin all around, looking for love in a world turned upside down.*

I had a dream last night, but something had changed.

The tables had turned, and inside my head burned with the aware-
ness and knowledge that life is for living and love is for loving
and songs are for singing—and in the midst of it all, my alarm
clock started ringing.

I arose from my bed, shook my head, and thought about the things I
had reaped, and then it dawned on me that I wasn't really asleep!

For the first time in my life, my eyes were wide open, and I was
aware and awake to the things that make life worth living and
time worth giving to the things that bring release and offer peace.

So, whether awake or asleep, dream of a life filled with songs for the
soul and love that makes whole whatever is broken.

Dream of hope and joy for better days ahead,

And when you dream, get out of your bed and bring to reality the
things that were said.

Dream again.

DESTINY'S CALLING

Look through the door of infinity and see destiny calling.

Smell the wind as it tickles your nose and blows open the door.

Walk into the place where time and space cease to be. Destiny is
waiting patiently.

Water falls and engulfs the air; cries of laughter are everywhere.

Singing and dancing, walking and prancing,

"Live life to the fullest," destiny is saying.

"No time for worry, doubt, or fear. It's time for love and living here."

Hours pass that seem like minutes floating on a cloud.

Time is spent, and the sun is no more.

Hesitantly I walk back through the door of infinity.

I glance back as destiny winks and blows a kiss.

With tears and a smile, I know I will miss this place.

Destiny is calling—can't you hear?

Walk into the place where time and space cease to be. Destiny is
waiting patiently.

GRAB THE WIND

I grabbed the wind in the palm of my hand.
I made a fist and held it real tight;
I kept it that way for most of the night.
Curiosity got the best of me, and I decided to take a peek and see
what the wind looked like as it sat in my hand.
I opened my hand very slowly, one finger at a time.
I looked for the wind, but the wind I couldn't find,
For as I opened my hand, the wind fled—whoosh—to the sky.
It left my grasp in the blink of an eye.
I didn't mind, you see, because I came to understand that not many
people can honestly say, "I held the wind in the palm of my hand!"
The power I felt for that brief moment made me cry. To think that I,
a mere mortal, could grab the wind!

MY BABY GIRL

When you came into my world, my life was a mess, and you know
that!
You showed up on the scene all sparkling and clean.
You were just what I needed to help me really believe that
It was time to take stock of my life.
You see, prior to your arrival, I was living like a wild girl, caught in
the cycle of addiction.
Baby girl, you taught me conviction!
All of sudden, I had another to think about.
It was through my love for you that Christ's love finally shined
through the muck and mire of my life.
Love for my baby girl!
You changed my world with one smile and a cry.

Even the diapers I would dry helped me to see life through different eyes.
I had purpose and destiny lying in my lap before me
As I dreamed of you and me taking life by storm
While wrapped in the capable arms of our Father who is in heaven.
So, as you live your life and grow, please always know that I was
      your first life's mission.
Mission accomplished, baby girl.
Thank you for changing my world!

POWERFUL

Crushing, rushing, majesty—the voice of the Lord speaks.
From the depths of the sea, the ocean is calling me to a place I have
      never been.
The power of the ocean surrounds me.
Crushing, rushing, majesty—the voice of the Lord speaks.
Inside me I hear the call of the sea; the ocean sings a melody of pow-
      erful possibilities.
I rock, I sway, and I'm lulled away as an infant in a cradle or a baby
      in the womb.
I am engulfed by the sea; the ocean speaks to me.
Crushing, rushing, majesty—the voice of the Lord speaks!

POWERFUL, PART 2

Crushing, rushing, majesty—the voice of the Lord speaks:
"I've taken you to the depths of the sea. Now I've hidden you in the
      cleft of the rock with Me.
"Now I show you who you were born to be, for today I set your mind free:
"Free to see My glory as My shadow engulfs you and you taste of My
      goodness that is marrow and health."
"This is the place of great wealth that comes not from man but only
      at My command.

"You may wonder why it has taken so long—but not very, for time
*   stands still when you live in Me and I live in you.*
"Today as yesterday and tomorrow as forever, I make all things new.
"The connecting of destiny to another takes time to be revealed and
*   healed from the breach and the break.*
"When I'm done, it's no longer fake but irreversibly real throughout
*   eternity."*
Crushing, rushing, majesty—the voice of the Lord speaks to me.
*   From the cleft of the rock by the sea, the Lord calls to me.*
Crushing, rushing, majesty—the voice of the Lord speaks!

Please visit http://bit.ly/PoemPowerful to see a video of Rosalind reciting
these poems on a beach in California.

Glossary

Mothers In Crisis, Inc. (MIC): 501(c)(3) nonprofit tax-exempt, charitable organization

Hope Universe Grace Initiative (HUGI): developed by MIC to carry out the task of establishing the Whole Hope Campaign

Christ Vision Tribe (CVT): the envisioning arm of MIC that meets weekly to strategize and organize ways to spread hope

Hope Squad: the team that goes out and implements events and activities designed to spread hope

HOPE: helping others practice empowerment

Hopeology: the study and practice of hope

Hopeologist: term trademarked with the US Patent and Trademark Office; promoting public awareness of hope by means of public advocacy. Hopeologist services consist of promoting Fridays as Hope Universe Day and April as the National Month of Hope.

Hope Universe Day: Fridays—a day to share hope and smiles

National Month of Hope: April—a month to celebrate and promote hope

think hope: choosing to look for the good in every challenging situation, focusing your thoughts on good things and believing that things can and will get better; looking for solutions; seeing hope like a light in dark tunnel that illuminates your path

hope connection: occurs when you bring hope to someone by connecting with your heart; can occur through hope chats, hope fusions, and hope spheres

hope chat: a one-on-one conversation with someone that brings hope to both him or her and you; requires seven steps (identify, prepare, go, listen, encourage, empower, and wrap up)

hope face: open and warm expression created when you look at someone and really see and connect with him or her; is kind, joyful, and nonjudgmental

hope fusion: occurs when you and another person continue to come together to share hope

hope sphere: created when three or more people come together in hope and each person begins to think hope, have hope chats, and participate in hope fusions; a place to cultivate a hopeful environment filled with love and encouragement

hope breaks: moments when you stop and intentionally think about good and hopeful things throughout your day in five-to-ten-minute increments

rest in hope: relaxing and trusting that God is with you and that everything will work out fine

Survey of Hope: consists of four questions (What is hope? What brings you hope or makes you feel hopeful? What are some things that zap your hope or make you feel less hope or hopeless? What do you experience when you are hopeful?)

symbols of hope: images, scents, living things, and other items that are often subtle but can create a more hopeful environment

spreading hope: sharing hope with others by doing things that will make a difference in their lives

Citizens of Hope Universe (COHs): individuals and organizations that support MIC's Whole Hope Campaign financially on a monthly basis; united in the belief that hope is a powerful force that can help people navigate challenging times

Go to www.rosalindytompkins.com and sign up for Rosalind Tompkins's newsletter and stay connected! Also, please join Mothers In Crisis, Inc. in the Campaign of Hope by becoming a Citizen of Hope Universe. Visit www.makeahopeconnection.com to become a Citizen of Hope today!

About the Author

Rosalind Y. Lewis Tompkins, whose trademarked moniker is Hopeologist, received an honorary doctorate of humanities from the Five-Fold Ministry Theological University in 2012 in recognition of the work she has done through Mothers In Crisis (MIC) to end drug and alcohol addiction and to relieve the suffering of families afflicted by these diseases. Dr. Tompkins founded MIC in April 1991. A 501(c)(3) federal tax-exempt nonprofit organization, it links families and communities to provide networks of support and to help families live productive, empowered, hope-filled lives. Through MIC, Dr. Tompkins has affected the lives of more than ten thousand families.

In June 2017, Dr. Tompkins was instrumental in designating April as National Month of Hope through the National Day Calendar. In keeping with her humanitarian call, Dr. Tompkins has traveled throughout the United States and around the world to spread hope to those most in need, including widows, orphans, and refugees. Her ministry has taken her to East, Central, and South Africa; Jamaica; the Dominican Republic; Haiti; and Turkey.

Dr. Tompkins is the author of *As Long as There Is Breath in Your Body, There Is Hope*; *Rare Anointing*; *You Are Beautiful: Unlocking Beauty from Within*; *What Is It? Defining, Finding, and Obtaining Your It*; and *Nimble Anointed Words Empower (N-AWE)*. With a firm belief that hope can change the world, Dr. Tompkins studies and spreads hope while empowering others to spread hope as they tap into their God-given power, potential, and purpose.

In addition, Dr. Tompkins:

- Was appointed by Governor Jeb Bush to the Commission for Volunteerism and Community Service for the state of Florida in 2006
- Is an empowerment life coach
- Is the lead pastor and founder of Turning Point International Church, the outreach chapel of MIC
- Is a Florida State University graduate known for her trademarked saying "As long as there is breath in your body, there is hope"
- Is a blogger and columnist for the *Tallahassee Democrat* newspaper

Dr. Tompkins is the wife of Elder Richard Lester Kwame Lewis, the mother of Janar Holloway, and the grandmother of Tayla, Mya, and Brian Holloway. She is well-known in the north Florida and south Georgia regions for her work with families and communities in crisis. For more information, visit www.rosalindytompkins.com.